WHAT WAS GOD DOING ON THE CROSS?

Jim Brandt

Trinity Seminary

CLASS

The Teaching Church & Theology

June 12 1995

D1251519

**Books by Alister McGrath published
by Zondervan . . .**

WHAT WAS GOD DOING ON THE CROSS?

ALISTER E. McGRATH

Zondervan Publishing House
Academic and Professional Books
Grand Rapids, Michigan

A Division of HarperCollinsPublishers

Requests for information should be addressed to:
Zondervan Publishing House
Academic and Professional Books
Grand Rapids, Michigan 49530

Cover design: Jack Foster Design
Cover illustration: Christ of St. John of the Cross, *Salva-
dor Dali. Glasgow Museum, Art Gallery and Museum,
Kelvingrove.*

Library of Congress Cataloging-in-Publication Data

McGrath, Alister E., 1953–
      What was God doing on the cross? / Alister E.
McGrath.
            p.   cm.
      Includes bibliographical references.
      ISBN 0-310-59451-0
      1. Holy Cross. 2. Jesus Christ—Crucifixion. 3.
Atonement.
      I. Title.
      BT453.M395   1992
      232.96'3–dc20   92-38943
                                                                  CIP

Printed in the United States of America

93 94 95 96 97 98 / EP / 10 9 8 7 6 5 4 3 2 1

Contents

Acknowledgments

This book is a greatly expanded version of a lecture given at Princeton Theological Seminary on 22 October 1990. In that lecture I began to explore ways of making the neglected and misunderstood classical approaches to the cross relevant to the needs of our own day and age. My thanks are due to Professor Diogenes Allen and President Thomas W. Gillespie for their hospitality on that occasion, and to the student audience who persuaded me that this book needed to be written. Juliet Newport rescued me from innumerable lapses in style and all too frequent use of theological jargon.

Making Sense of the Cross

T he cross stands at the heart of the Christian faith. But what does it mean? How can we make sense of it? Many Christians feel that wrestling with the full meaning of the cross could bring a new quality and depth to their faith. They believe that they have caught only a glimpse of the insights to be gained from the cross. They are looking for someone to point them to the richness of the Christian understanding of the cross of Christ. They long for the treasure chest to be unlocked, and its scintillating contents laid out for all to behold.

If you have ever had this feeling, this book is for you. It is an attempt to allow the cross to speak to us as if for the very first time. It tries to recover the newness of faith, breathing fresh air into what has often become a very stale discussion. It aims to set out, simply yet not simplistically, the riches of the Christian understanding of the cross. Its method is thoroughly traditional. Like an explorer who walks around the base of a great mountain, surveying its slopes from different aspects, this book presents different perspectives on the cross of Christ. It makes no claims whatsoever to originality. Its goal has been to make accessible the treasury of Christian insights concerning the crucifixion and resurrection of Jesus Christ. It is written with the needs of ordinary Christians, and those who minister to them, kept firmly in mind. These insights are your heritage; this book has been written in order that you may lay claim to them, and in doing so, deepen your faith and understanding.

What If He *Was* God?

We are standing on the second wall of the ancient city of Jerusalem on a late spring morning. The passover is just about to begin, as the people of God recall God's faithfulness to his covenant. The passover lambs are being prepared for slaughter inside the city. Yet this great festival is marred by the knowledge that Jerusalem is no longer a free city. The city and the surrounding area are under Roman occupation, and they have been for some time.

The Romans are unpopular. Although many of the local population are prepared to tolerate their rule, many dream of independence and the restoration of nationhood. They talk about the coming of the kingdom of God, and the long-awaited arrival of a redeemer who will deliver them from bondage. Every now and then, those dreams explode into action. Rebellion breaks out. As often as it breaks out, it is ruthlessly suppressed by the Romans, and its leaders executed.

They call the preferred way of execution 'crucifixion'. The word, which sounds neat and clinical in its precision, refers to nothing other than legalized sadism. It is probably one of the most depraved forms of execution ever devised. It is nothing other than death by slow torture. It works. No-one has ever survived a crucifixion before. It certainly deters others from resisting the Romans. There is nothing like a row of crucified corpses, displayed for everyone to see along the public highway, to bring home the inevitable results of rebellion.

Everyone knows what happens. They have been told often enough, and many have seen it for themselves. They begin by stripping the victim to the waist, and whipping him. Not with an ordinary whip, of course: it has broken pieces of bone or little pieces of rough metal tied to its ends. It tears the victims' backs to shreds. Then they make them carry their own crosses to the place of execution. There are different types of crosses, but they all have the same basic structure. There is a kind of heavy crossbar, which the Romans call a *patibulum*, attached to the main upright beam. And this is what they make the victims carry to the local place of execution. (Someone with a grim sense of humour called it 'the place of the skull'.) It exhausts them – and it's meant to.

When they get them there, they strip them. That usually gets a few laughs from the crowds. Why is it that public executions attract people? Adding public humiliation to physical pain makes crucifixion especially degrading, and adds to its deterrent effect. Then they raise them up on the cross. Usually they nail them through the wrists; if you nail them through the hands, they fall off, and you have to start again. There's a device that stops them falling off, called a *sedile* – a sort of small seat, about halfway up the main beam of the cross. It also stops them from dying too soon. It becomes too painful for them to breathe. Eventually, the effort is just too much, and they collapse, and die of suffocation.

It is a horrifying and pitiful scene, even by the tragic standards of this grim and cynical world. Even the passover lambs are killed more humanely than this. One quick cut, and it's all over; the agony of death is kept to a minimum. When they crucify someone, they want to prolong the agony. However, there have to be limits to the length of time it takes to crucify people. The executioners couldn't be expected to be there beyond nightfall. So the Romans devised a neat way of speeding up the process – a sort of *coup de grâce*. They broke the victims' legs. Suddenly, they couldn't hold themselves up any longer. The pressure on their chests became unbearable. Death followed quickly, as their lungs collapsed.

And, as we watch, such a pathetic scene seems to be happening in front of our eyes. Three victims are stumbling past, each bent double under the excruciating weight of the crossbar. One of them seems to be in a really bad way; in fact, he's just collapsed. The soldiers grab a bystander, and make him carry it instead. Now they have come to the place of execution. They are stripping them of their clothes, and nailing them to the crosses. It is a sickening sight. Yet the crowds seem to love it. They are shouting what seems to be all kind of abuse at them – at least, at one of them in particular. Isn't there meant to be something special about one of them?

He was a carpenter, they say. Now there's a real irony for you. A carpenter being crucified – killed by his own handiwork. The creator being destroyed by

his own creation, as it were. But why bother cru-
cifying a carpenter? The other two are criminals of
some kind. Some say that they are Zealots, the revolu-
tionaries that want to do away with Roman rule. But
the third man – well, he's being treated as if he were a
criminal, but he seems to be different. Who was he?
And how did he come to be here?

They say he was a teacher – that he taught with
authority. But that's hardly a reason for him being
there. Nobody ever said that he taught rebellion
against the Romans. In fact, they say that he distanced
himself from the Zealots. There must be more to it
than this. Of course, some say that he made outrageous claims about himself. They say that he claimed to
be able to forgive sins. Everyone knows that only God
can forgive sins. Perhaps he was claiming to be God?

Well, you can see why people wouldn't like that.
Suppose that God came down to earth and showed us
what he thought of people's pathetic little theories
about him. Imagine how annoyed the theologians
would get! All that talk about God being far off and
distant. All of that would have to go! If this man was
God, it would be like dropping some kind of bomb-
shell in the theologians' playground. It would spoil all
their fun. Just look at the pain that this man is suffering. Whoever heard of a suffering God? The idea is
plain daft. God is up there in heaven, and there he will
stay.

But wouldn't it be wonderful if it were true? If God
came to visit us, like a great king visiting his subjects.
Or, even better, if he came among us as one of us,
sharing our way of life, with all its tragedy, sorrows
and grief! Wouldn't it be amazing to be able to touch
him? To see him? To be able to meet God in the form
of a person? It would completely transform our way of

thinking about God. But it can't be right. It's just wishful thinking. After all, if this man was God, what is he doing on the cross?

Everyone knows that God is all-powerful. So what would he be doing at a squalid little scene like this? Think of the humiliation! If God is so clever, he could have got out of this. The very fact that this man has ended up on a cross is the ultimate proof that he isn't God. And what's more, there are rumours spreading that he's just cried out something about being abandoned by God. Well, there's proof, if it were needed.

Anyway, everyone seems agreed that he was a really good religious teacher. So he can't have gone round the place claiming to be God, or to do the sort of things that only God can do – that would be megalomania. It would end his credibility as a religious leader. Even if he just did things or said things which *implied* that he was God, then we could not take him seriously as a teacher.

Now if he *was* God – well, we'd listen to him rather carefully then. For a start, he'd be telling us about God at first hand. All the rest of us have to speculate at second hand. After all, nobody has ever seen God. It's not as if some people have a hotline to God. It's not as if they know exactly what he is like and what he wants us to do. We're all in the same boat. It would be really rather threatening if he was different – if he knew something that the rest of us didn't. That would put the professional theologians' noses out of joint. Imagine the humiliation if a carpenter knew more about God than they did. (Maybe we can understand why the theologians wanted him crucified, after all!)

But he can't have been God. The idea of God becoming a human being – well, that's just absurd. Everyone knows that you can't be God and a human being at one and the same time. God would get himself tied in all sorts of logical knots if he tried to do that. There's nothing like a good dose of logic for sorting out these theological problems.

But who was he, then? He must have been more than a teacher. It's all something of a mystery, rather like one of those detective novels, except that whodunnits try to work out who did the murder. (There is no mystery about who is killing this man, after all – it's the Romans, isn't it?) What we have here is more of a who-is-it, a mystery about the identity of the person who's being killed, rather than the one who did the killing. What we need are some clues.

We could begin by exploring his background. They say he came from Nazareth. Well, that's hardly a promising start. Is anything big going to start at Nazareth? And then there were those rumours about his birth. That he didn't have a proper father, or something. Some say he was the result of an affair between some low-ranking Roman soldier and a Jewish girl. Well, that just makes things worse.

But then there are the other rumours. That he came from Bethlehem in Judea. Now that town has a long-standing connection with the ancient Israelite royal family. Could he be a new king of Israel? After all, there's that notice nailed above him. 'The king of the Jews,' it says. But maybe they're just poking fun at him, to humiliate him. Look at that crown of thorns they've given him.

Maybe he was some kind of religious prophet. After all, there was all that fuss about that other man a couple of years ago, the one who started baptizing people in the wilderness around the river Jordan a few years back. They called him John the Baptist. Some thought that he marked the beginning of a new era in the history of the people of God. They thought that God was going to speak to them in some spectacular new way. But John had this idea that he was just a forerunner, that someone big was going to come after him. That got them really excited. There was something about God sending a messenger ahead of him to prepare his way. If this guy was the messenger ... well, you can see why people thought that something big was about to happen. I mean, God visiting his people. Actually being present among them. That would be incredible. But the shabby scene being acted out today puts paid to that story. No sign of God out there.

But then there were the other things. Those parables that man on the cross told the crowds. It wasn't just that he taught them with authority. It was that they seemed to be expecting someone to teach them in this way – someone special. And they say that he healed people – the lame, the deaf, the blind and the dumb. And that seemed to mean something to them. It was almost as if they were awaiting someone just like this.

And they called him Jesus. Now that's another thing. Jesus means 'God saves'. They seem to have expected God to do something big through him – like saving his people. But they say that it was his own people who rejected and despised him. Now that doesn't make sense. If this man was the long-awaited figure that everyone's been waiting for, why hand him over to be executed in this way? He can't be the Messiah. Everyone knows that the Messiah is a triumphant hero, who will liberate his people from their bondage to the Romans. And there have been others, like Theudas and Judas the Galilean, all claiming to be messiahs. Look what happened to them. Look what happened to Jesus. Mind you, they asked Jesus if he was the Messiah. He didn't answer them. He was silent before his accusers. Some people seem to think that was significant.

But there he is now, abandoned by his followers. They say one of them denied publicly having anything to do with him. He even seems to be abandoned by God. In fact, they are saying that he died cursed by God. It was something to do with the way in which he died, hanging on a tree. What an end. To have to die in such pain, mocked by the taunting crowds, and abandoned by your friends and your God.

As we watch, the sun begins to set over the place of execution. It is now the eve of the Sabbath, the day when God rested from his labours in creating the world. As the shadows get longer, the Roman soldiers look at each other, and seem to exchange some kind of signal. They break the legs of the two men on either side. They do something different to the man in the middle. He has been still for a long time. Perhaps he is already dead? They don't bother to break his legs. Instead, they stab him with a spear, opening up a deep wound. Even from here, we can see the blood. It seems to be coagulated. If he wasn't dead before, he certainly is now. Dust to dust, and all that. Still, it has to happen to us all. There's nothing that can be done about it. It is a shame that this man had to go in such a dreadful way.

Whoever it was dying on that cross, he has been well and truly killed. These Romans certainly know how to make sure that someone is dead. We shall not be hearing from him again. Or his followers, poor deluded fools that they were. They say that they left everything to follow this Jesus. Now he is dead, and what have they got to show for it? Their hopes and their lives have been shattered. As we turn away, a pathetic little group of people carry off his body into the distance, disappearing into the blackness of the falling night.

Hallucination or Vindication?

D istressed by the shocking scenes of that dismal Friday, we leave Jerusalem for the hill country of Judea, exploring some of the famous sights of the region. A few days later, we return to Jerusalem. It is now nearly a week after the death of the man they called Jesus of Nazareth. Inside the city, there appears to be some excitement. There is a rumour spreading furiously to the effect that Jesus is not dead after all. They say that he has been raised from the dead. People are electrified by the suggestion. Of course, you can hardly expect any better from superstitious people. They're bound to believe some incredible story like that. Anyway, everyone expects resurrections to happen round here, so it would be very easy for them to believe that this man has been raised again.

On second thoughts, however, this doesn't make as much sense as we thought at first. If people round here expected resurrections to happen, they would take place right at the end of history. Yet they are telling us that Jesus has actually been raised here in Jerusalem. And history hasn't ended yet. Life is still going on. This doesn't fit a common pattern at all. It is way out of line with expectations. It has broken the mould of existing beliefs. And the people around here are so conservative that it would take something spectacular to make them change their minds about just about anything, let alone something so big. Maybe there is something in these rumours, after all?

But if they were true, these rumours would be politically explosive. It would be very bad news for the Romans if the man people called the 'king of the Jews' were to have come back from the dead. It might spark off a revolt. People would argue that God was on their side. That they were invincible. So why don't the Roman authorities put paid to these rumours? Why don't they just produce the corpse of this man Jesus? That would be more than enough to discredit these stories, once and for all. This would end this speculation about some kind of resurrection.

After all, it just doesn't make sense. People don't rise from the dead. It's never happened before. Some people round here say that the dead descend to Sheol. They say it's a kind of gloomy pit which is nothing like the world of the living, where you lose touch with God altogether. Others say that there will be a resurrection right at the end of history, when the dead will be gloriously raised to life once more. But that seems a long way ahead. There are also some mysterious references to God acting in some wonderful way to restore his people 'on the third day'. But nobody seems to be sure quite what they mean. And some – the Sadducees – are quite clear that there is no resurrection at all. So the death of Jesus can only be bad news. Except for Barabbas, that is. After all, Jesus died instead of him.

Of course, there were those old stories about Egyptian or Greek gods dying and rising again. There was Adonis, who was meant to have been accidentally killed while hunting boar, but was allowed to return from the underworld for six months in the year. But that bears no resemblance to the rumours about Jesus. In any case, the stories about Egyptian deities were just myths. Nobody ever believed that sort of thing really happened. They never tell us *when* they are meant to have happened. They never tell us *where* they happened. And they never tell us *who* saw what happened. But some of these people out there are claiming that this man Jesus was raised from the dead, right here in Jerusalem. More than that, they insist that they were witnesses to the fact. Around here, they say that if two men are witnesses to an event, that's enough to clinch it.[1] And there seem to be a dozen or so of them out there, each claiming to be a witness to this so-called resurrection.

But they seem to have mishandled their public relations. Apparently these people are claiming that the first witnesses to this resurrection were women. But everyone knows that the witness of a woman is worth nothing. You would think that they would have thought about that when they invented their absurd story. As it stands, it is quite incredible; it might have been a bit more credible (but not much) if they had rewritten the story a little. Why have women as key witnesses?

But we all know that resurrections just do not happen. After all, nobody has ever seen anyone rise from the dead. It would be different if we knew about other people who had been raised from the dead. It would

23

make it much easier to believe what these men and women are telling us happened. There is nothing like precedents to make something easier to accept. Suppose that we saw people rising from the dead left, right and centre. Well, we would have no problems in believing that Jesus had been raised from the dead as well, would we?

Mind you, if resurrections happened regularly, there would be nothing *different* about Jesus being raised from the dead. He would be one among many, just another statistic. That would hardly explain the excitement out there. They believe it is something unique. If it *is* unique, then, by definition, there will be no analogous events. That makes it a lot harder to believe. It also makes it worth believing. If it did happen, it would be quite amazing. It would certainly explain the excitement with which these followers of Jesus are going round the place, proclaiming that he is risen.

It would be easy to dismiss the resurrection if these people had been expecting their Jesus to be raised from the dead. But they were obviously traumatized by his death. They seem to have believed that his death on the cross marked the end of his life and their faith. They just were not looking for something dramatic and unexpected to take place. In fact, they seem to have had some difficulty in accepting that the tomb was empty in the first place. And it isn't just the empty tomb which has led them to believe that their Jesus has been raised from the dead. They claim to have seen him. They tell us that they have encountered him.

And another thing. People here like to pay great respect to their dead heroes. Their great King David died, and his tomb is still there in Jerusalem, the site of much religious devotion. They worship at the tombs of their prophets.[2] But there is not even a hint of that

24

with these people who followed Jesus during his lifetime. They don't seem to have the slightest interest in his tomb. All they seem interested in is this risen Jesus. Indeed, they sum up their good news in the words, 'He is risen.'

Of course, they say that Jesus raised people from the dead. There was that episode with Jairus's daughter.[3] And there was that business about Lazarus,[4] which kept the gossips busy for weeks. But that was really just some kind of temporary resuscitation. Lazarus was brought back to life. His death was just postponed. But when they talk about Jesus being raised from the dead, they seem to believe Jesus will never die again. They are saying that Jesus is the conqueror of death. It's almost as if it was death itself which died on that cross.

But there is more to it than this. Suppose Jesus has been raised from the dead. He will have broken free from the bounds of time and space. It will mean that anyone at any time will be able to encounter him. You could be walking down some road or other, miles away from Jerusalem, minding your own business, and be confronted by him. And it won't be just the inhabitants of Judea in the first half of this century who will encounter him. He will be available to all in history. That's just incredible. The way would be clear for this man to have a bigger impact on history than anyone else who has ever lived. Before you know what is happening, they will be dating history from *his* birth, instead of some more important event, like the founding of the great city of Rome.

But it can't have happened. It is all a simple misunderstanding. These credulous peasants are the victims of some hysterical delusion. It's just wish-fulfilment. These people cannot cope with the fact that this man Jesus claimed to be someone special, and then was executed. He is as dead as dead can be. The Romans made sure of that. They are bound to display his corpse publicly. That will sort things out.

But, on second thoughts, this mass-delusion theory doesn't really seem very convincing. The language is all wrong. These people keep on saying, 'He appeared to us.'[5] They refuse to use language that could imply that they just had some kind of subjective individualistic experience of his presence. The emphasis is not on the person who sees Jesus – it is on the fact that Jesus makes himself known to his disciples. They keep on stressing the objective nature of the resurrection. It's something that happened in the real world, not just inside their heads.

These people saw something which made them think that Jesus was alive again. A hallucination just doesn't make sense. They obviously saw Jesus in a recognizable form. The neatest explanation would be that Jesus wasn't really dead in the first place. His crucifixion may have been a botched job. Admittedly, this would be rather unusual. The Romans were usually careful about the way in which they executed people. They made sure that they were dead by the end of the day, having suffered as much as possible in the meantime. And you would think that they might have taken especial care over this man. Think of the claims that people were making about him. It would be asking for trouble to fail to kill him properly.

The most likely explanation is that he fainted on the cross. It was a hot day; he was exhausted from the pain of crucifixion. It would be quite understandable if he collapsed under all that strain. The executioners would just assume that he was dead, and fail to check him out properly. They would have buried him while he was still alive, thinking that he was dead.

It's easy to work out what happened next. He would have been placed in the coolness of the tomb. Maybe the fragrance of the embalming spices would have revived him. Anyway, he would have come back to consciousness. He would have left the tomb. And people would assume that he had come back to life. These reports about appearances to his followers are very persistent, so they would have to be based on *something*. It makes sense.

Mind you, you would have to be remarkably credulous to think he had come back from the dead. How could anyone look at someone half dead from crucifixion, and think he had come back from the dead? How could someone who had not eaten for days and had lost a huge amount of blood from all those wounds pass himself off as the conqueror of death? He wouldn't have been able to walk, let alone persuade people that he had vanquished the final enemy of humanity. It stretches the imagination to breaking point. He would have died of exhaustion shortly afterwards, a victim of the death he had claimed to defeat – but which in reality had defeated him. Nobody could be so foolish as to believe that. Nobody would want to *worship* someone like that. There would have to be something remarkable about Jesus to persuade people that he had really risen from the dead, rather than just postponed his death.

Perhaps there has been some kind of mix-up about the tomb. Maybe people got muddled about where Jesus was buried. After all, it is quite possible that someone may have decided to remove Jesus from his tomb, and bury him somewhere more dignified.[6] But that doesn't really explain the way these people have been changed. At the time of his trial and execution, they were just a bunch of cowering failures. Everyone knows that. Their leader even denied publicly having anything to do with Jesus. And now they seem filled with confidence. They have been transformed. That takes some explaining. But time will put an end to this story; you can't keep a myth going for long. After a few months, they will tire of keeping up the pretence of having seen Jesus, risen from the dead. And their movement will peter out.

But what if it were true? Suppose Jesus really had risen from the dead . . . wouldn't it turn our world and ways of thinking inside out? That someone real and living – not one of these mythological characters – had finally broken the bonds of death? That someone had gone to Sheol, and come back? Suppose it were true – what would its implications be?

Take that idea of God acting in some wonderful way 'on the third day'. Didn't God tell Abraham to sacrifice his son – and yet on the third day he provided a substitute sacrifice, so that his son might live?[7] Was it not on the third day that Joshua led the people of Israel into the promised land? Didn't this signal a vital new period in the history of the people of God, and fulfil a long-standing promise?[8] And was there not that mysterious prophetic promise, by which God pledged himself to restore his people, and raise them up, on the third day?[9] Might not the resurrection of Jesus be a great act of divine deliverance?

And what about his death on the cross? People said it showed that he died cursed by God.[10] Yet if Jesus was raised from the dead by God, might not God be overturning that verdict? Might he not be publicly vindicating Jesus? Perhaps God was stamping all that Jesus said and did with his seal of approval? The resurrection would certainly single out Jesus as someone unique in his relationship with God. Nobody else has been exalted and raised in this way before.[11] Jesus would have been given a new status in the eyes of the world – one who had been raised to glory. The whole meaning of what happened on the cross would have to be thought through all over again. People said it meant that Jesus had been condemned by God. But in the light of the resurrection, that idea drops dead. So what *does* the cross mean, then? A long process of wrestling with the cross would lie ahead. It could have some very exciting results.

For a start, the resurrection would then be telling us something about the identity of Jesus. People expected the resurrection to happen right at the end of history. That would be the moment when the dead were raised and judged by God. And then the glory of God would finally be revealed.[12] But the resurrection of Jesus has been shifted from the end of time to our own history. It has happened right now. And that must mean that these other things are also happening – the judgment of the world, and the revelation of the glory of God. Could it be that the resurrection – or even the risen Christ himself – is judging us? That the glory of God is being revealed in the resurrection of Jesus? That would mean that Jesus and God were . . . well, were both on the same level, so to speak. It would mean that Jesus was doing things which God alone can do – save us, judge us, and reveal the divine glory.

Yet that is precisely what they said Jesus was doing, even before his death. They say that he claimed to forgive human sin – something that only God can do. Maybe the resurrection is telling us that he was meant to. Maybe we are meant to read the story of Jesus all over again, in that light.

Then there was what John the Baptist said – that he

had come to prepare the way for the Lord.[13] And
everyone got excited. They knew their prophecies,
and were watching out for God to come and visit and
redeem his people. Then Jesus suddenly appears on the
scene. And John seems to have been expecting that. He
seems to have known something about Jesus – something that made him hesitate before baptizing him.
That seems significant. It was as if he knew that Jesus
didn't *need* to be baptized. It was as if he had no sin to
be washed away. If anybody needed to baptize anyone
else, it was John who needed to be baptized by Jesus.[14]
Or there was that amazing scene when Jesus claimed to
have authority to forgive sins.[15] It caused an outrage at
the time. Everyone – including Jesus himself – knew
that only God can forgive sins. After the cross, that
claim seemed absurd, even blasphemous. But now,
after the resurrection . . . well, it has to be seen in a
new light. The man who some thought to be a deluded
egomaniac turns out to have been vindicated by the
highest authority!

What seemed ridiculous if Jesus was just a man
makes perfect sense if he really was God. In his words
and his deeds, Jesus seems to have expressed his belief
that God was at work within him – and more than
that. Jesus conveyed the impression that he had the
authority to act and speak as God.[16] It is almost as if he
anticipated the verdict of the resurrection – that he was
authorized to speak and act in this way. And didn't
people say that he taught with authority?[17]

Suppose it were true. What would it tell us about
God? Or about Jesus? Or about ourselves? If Jesus is
God, it means that we have a revelation of God which
goes far beyond anything and everything we have ever
had in the past. Before Jesus, God was able to speak to
us in all sorts of ways – such as through the history of

his people Israel, through his servant Moses, and through the great prophets. But all that was at second hand. It was other people telling us about what God was like. Other people told us what God wanted us to do or believe. It wasn't as if God came among his people personally, and told them about himself at first hand. And if he was to do that – well, he would have to do it as a person, wouldn't he? Otherwise he wouldn't be able to communicate with us.

If Jesus is God, it means that God has spoken to us directly. It means that the great gulf between God and ourselves has been bridged. We don't have to climb up some spiritual ladder to find God. He has come down to meet us where we are. And he doesn't leave us there. He takes us back up that ladder with him. God has come down to our level, to speak to us in person. We could really trust what Jesus told us about God, because he would have inside knowledge, denied to everyone else in history.

And it would mean that any idea of God as some distant and remote figure would have to go. We had always thought of God as standing aloof from his creation, but if Jesus is God, then we will have to revise that completely. The creator chose to enter into his creation. What humility that would show! It would be like the Roman emperor setting aside his palaces and good food in Rome, and living in the slums of Judea for a couple of years!

It would also mean that we could begin to picture God in our minds in a way never possible before. We would be able to talk with confidence about God in memorable ways. We wouldn't be at a loss for words when trying to talk about God. We could point to this man Jesus, and say, 'God is like that.' People have always found it very difficult to talk about the love of

God. They usually end up by saying that it is indescribable. That may well be true, but it isn't very helpful to anyone who wants to have it described to them! But now we can begin to speak about that love in a powerful way. We could say that the love of God is like that of a man who willingly gives up his life, so that his friend can live.[18] And we have been authorized to speak like this! It is as if God had said, 'I want you to talk about me in this way. Look at Jesus. *I'm* like that!'

Of course, the sceptics won't like this very much. 'God cannot become human,' they'll say. 'The textbooks don't allow for it.' Well, the textbooks will just have to be rewritten. And they will say that it is undignified for God to share in the suffering of his people. Well, that idea will have to be challenged as well. Where do they get these ideas from, anyway?[19] Who says that God cannot suffer? If Jesus suffered, then God suffered as well. And that's another thing. Suppose God knows at first hand what it is like to suffer. It would be a lot easier for us to pray to him when we suffer, wouldn't it? We wouldn't have to explain to him what human suffering was like, or what it's like to be betrayed by friends, or to be abandoned when the going gets tough. He already knows that. He's been this way before us. And so we could turn to him in the sure knowledge that he knows and understands. Now that makes prayer different.

And what about us? What about our situation? We are born to die. It all seems so pointless. Everything that you live for is going to be taken away from you. It's almost as if it is all a waste of time. The old-timers say that you can know God during your lifetime. Then you disappear into some God-forsaken pit, and you might well end up never experiencing him again. It all seems so bleak and hopeless. It's not surprising that people don't like the idea of death very much.

In fact, the crucifixion of Jesus seems to sum up everything that is wrong with the world. There seems to be no justice. Why should someone wonderful like Jesus be executed? If they kill people like him, what hope is there for the rest of us? And the sickening way in which they killed him shows up the depths of sadism that lie just beneath the surface of human nature. The execution of Jesus – the one person who *deserved* to live – somehow seems to stand as a symbol of all that is wrong with the world. On its own, the cross is just a symbol of despair and hopelessness.

But if Jesus was raised from the dead, that symbol of despair becomes a symbol of hope. It would stand for the hope that is born in the world's darkest hour, when all seemed to be lost and beyond repair. It would represent the birth of joy on the far side of despair. The cross would show up the futility of basing hope upon our own human resources. The resurrection would show that God can bring hope where no others can. And that hope is no pious sentiment, uttered bravely but without foundation. Rather, it is hard-headed realism. It is grounded in the overwhelming sense of exhilaration which gradually seems to have dawned among those who witnessed the crucifixion. The one who had been killed before them was dead no more. And with this defeat of death, a new phase in human history would be born. Perhaps an empty cross could symbolize this divine juxtaposition of despair and hope?

It would be wonderful if it were true. Even the *idea* that God should become like one of us, and share our human story, is just too wonderful for words. It would do more than change our ways of thinking about God; it would change our lives, by giving us new reasons to hope and believe while we live in this crazy and hopeless world. But it can't be true. Enough of daydreaming. Any minute now, the authorities will produce the corpse of Jesus. Then all this speculation will die down, and we will hear no more of this man. And as for those thoughts about God and ourselves? They were just another false dawn in the world's dark night. Sadly, they can never be anything more than wishful thinking. A pity. They were very exciting – while they lasted. And we wait, gloomily, for the corpse of the man they called Jesus of Nazareth to be publicly displayed. And wait . . .

The period of waiting has become days. There is a growing sense of excitement. The resurrection rumour could be discredited totally by one single action – producing the body of the crucified Christ. But it is embarrassingly absent. And people are noticing. For the resurrection is set to change everything. If Jesus really has been raised from the dead, then maybe there is hope for all of us. Maybe he is some kind of trailblazer, cutting out a path down which the rest of us can travel. Maybe he has broken down some kind of barrier, so that we can pass through to something new and wonderful.

But how? How could we connect up with what he has done? How could we share in this hope of resurrection after death? Just imagine if, having begun to know God in this life, we could continue that relationship afterwards. It would be as if we had begun something which nothing could break or destroy – something that we could hold on to. And if the power of death has been broken, then what about all the other old enemies? What about sin, which traps us and holds us in its grim grasp, from which we cannot break free by ourselves? Something very significant might well

34

have been going on there on that cross, unnoticed and unsuspected by those who watched Jesus of Nazareth die. This could be the beginning of something very big . . .

Some Things Are More Than They Seem

Christianity affirms that Jesus Christ really died, and that he really rose again. This is no wishful thinking – this is hard historical fact. If those events did not happen, then the credentials of Christianity are destroyed. Yet the gospel is about more than simply declaring the facts of history. It is not so much the *events* of the crucifixion and resurrection themselves, as their *significance* which lies at the heart of the Christian faith. That Jesus died is history; that Jesus died *for our sins* is the gospel.[20]

We can begin to explore this point by looking at an incident from Roman history. Forty-nine years before Christ was born, Julius Caesar led an army southwards from modern-day France. At one point, they had to cross a river – the Rubicon. Crossing it posed no particular difficulties, and required no acts of heroism. It was not like crossing a wide and raging torrent, such as those encountered by the American settlers, as they moved westwards. The mere act of crossing the Rubicon was of no historical significance. But that river happened to mark the border of the territory governed directly by the Roman senate. As a result, crossing this international boundary line was nothing less than a declaration of war by Caesar against Rome. One of the most famous civil wars in history began with that seemingly insignificant event.

But only someone in the know at the time would realize the full implications of what Caesar had done. Everyone else would simply have noticed a small army of men crossing a rather unimportant river. People cross rivers every day of the week. There is nothing special even about armies crossing a river. Things like that are a regular part of the staple diet of military training.

We need therefore to establish not just what happened, but how that event should be interpreted. The principle is the same, whether we are dealing with Caesar crossing the Rubicon, or Jesus dying upon the cross and rising again from the dead. The historical significance of the event needs to be settled. It is this process which can be seen at work in the New Testament, especially the writings of Paul.

At first, the early preaching of the apostles resonates with a simple theme – he is risen! The one who was crucified has been raised from the dead. The sheer joy of this realization dominates the early sermons in the Acts of the Apostles. But gradually, we see sustained reflection beginning to take place. What else does the resurrection mean? How are we to make sense of the cross, in the light of the resurrection? One immediate interpretation of the cross – that Jesus died under divine condemnation – was totally discredited by the resurrection. The resurrection reversed and overturned the judgment of

Jesus' opponents. So what sort of insights concerning Jesus did the resurrection point to?

We may pick out a few, before moving on.[21] First, the resurrection demonstrated that Jesus – the one who had been crucified – was now Lord. 'Let all Israel be assured of this: God has made this Jesus, whom you crucified, both Lord and Christ' (Acts 2:36). The word 'Lord' is of enormous importance. In the first place, it points to the ideas of authority and sovereignty. The resurrection endows Jesus with an authority which was present, but publicly unacknowledged, during his ministry. The secret of the identity and authority of Jesus is now publicly revealed. The resurrection declares that Jesus has authority to act and speak as God – and thus retrospectively validates his claims to such authority during his ministry. In other words, to give one example, Jesus' claim to be able to forgive sins, which rightly caused such offence among his audience (after all, only God can forgive sins!),[22] is seen to have rested upon secure foundations, even if these were not fully recognized at the time.

So who was Jesus? The resurrection shows up as shallow and inadequate any attempt to make sense of Jesus simply in terms of a good religious teacher. Here is one who acts as God, who speaks as God, and who represents and reveals God. 'Anyone who has seen me has seen the Father' (John 14:9). The New Testament summarizes this stunning insight by referring to Jesus as the Son of God. As Paul puts it, Jesus 'was declared with power to be the Son of God by his resurrection from the dead' (Romans 1:4). The use of the images of Father and Son to refer to God and Jesus Christ within the New Testament is enormously important. It represents an attempt to *distinguish* Jesus from God, while at the same time declaring that they are both divine. The resurrection demonstrates the divinity of Christ – one of the most thrilling themes of the New Testament and Christian faith. This insight is often stated in terms of 'the doctrine of the incarnation' – in other words, that God became one of us – a human being – in Jesus Christ.[23]

For if Jesus *is* God, then an array of remarkable insights about God assemble in front of us, each of them worthy of a book in itself. Two of these insights may be considered, before we move on. First, it is notoriously difficult to speak about God, partly because we find it hard to picture him. Very often 'God' is little more than an abstract idea. But if Jesus is God, then we are suddenly presented with the best visual aid for God the world has ever known. Jesus is the visual aid which God has given to us, and which he wants us to use. To have seen Jesus is to have seen the Father.

The New Testament declares that the love of God can be seen in the death of Christ. It is an amazing insight, a vital resource for evangelism, and one of the most treasured possessions of the Christian church. But it rests upon the divinity of Christ. Suppose Jesus Christ is *not* God, but just a man. Then the cross shows the love of one human being for others. It is human, not divine, love. The cross shows the love of God for us, because it is the Son of God who went to the cross for us. Lose sight of the divinity of Christ, and the full depth of meaning of the cross is diluted. We would have only half a redeemer.

The doctrine of the incarnation speaks movingly not only of the love of God, but of his *humility*. The creator of the world chose to enter into his world, not as a Roman emperor at the seat of imperial power, but as a child born in squalor somewhere in a far corner of the empire. God humbled himself, stooping down to meet us where we are – and we must humble ourselves, if we are to meet him.

So the events of the crucifixion and resurrection tell us about the nature of God. But they do more than this. If the first sermons in Acts are dominated by the proclamation of the *reality* of the resurrection, then the later writings are dominated by reflection on the *meaning* of the cross. Jesus Christ has been raised for us and for our salvation. For the crucifixion and resurrection can never be separated. The resurrection breaks down the barrier of secrecy concerning the identity of the man they crucified. The Son of God suffered and died at Calvary. Why should the world listen to this? And how can it benefit from it?

These are among the most important and central questions that Christian theology has to wrestle with. The resurrection shows us that Jesus is divine. It tells us the identity of the man who died upon the cross. It makes clear that this was no ordinary man, but God incarnate. Knowing who is being crucified, what new insights can we glean from Calvary? How can the cross change things?

The cross changes lives

Why is it that theology textbooks are often among the most tedious books ever written? As a university teacher of theology, I often find myself acutely embarrassed by this question. I do not exclude myself when I ask, 'If Christianity is so wonderful, how come its thinkers often manage to make it so wearisome and dull?'

One answer to this question might be that the kind

ple who write textbooks often have little con-
with the everyday life and worship of Chris-
So they get cut off from the sense of vibrancy
which is the powerhouse of Christian living. But I
think there is another reason. Too often, Christianity
is presented as if it were just about theories. It is treated
as if it were some kind of philosophy, appealing only
to academics.

But the reason why Christianity keeps going is that
it possesses the ability to change peoples' lives. The
way in which people are changed by Christ makes us
want to understand the meaning of the cross. Theologians develop theories about the cross because they
have to explain how and why the cross is able to have
such a powerful and transforming effect upon people.

The New Testament itself chronicles the effect that
the cross and resurrection of Christ have upon people.
Peter, Mary and Paul are individuals whose lives are
changed totally and irreversibly by these events. This
list could be extended enormously by an appeal to the
history of Christianity. It includes people like ourselves. We were not there at Calvary. We know it only
through faith. Yet the cross has turned our lives inside
out. But how could this happen? What resources and
potential must there be in the cross and resurrection of
Jesus, if it has this sort of effect upon people? Simplifi-
cations are dangerous, but there is some truth in the
simple suggestion that the gospels are mainly
interested in telling us about the effect that Jesus has
upon people, while Paul's letters are more interested in
explaining *how* he is able to have such an effect. The
gospels are about the facts. Paul provides the theory to
explain those facts.

Just about every theology textbook has a section
dealing with ways of making sense of the cross. The

rather clumsy phrase 'theories of the atonement' is often used. I often wish that this phrase could be abandoned completely, for two reasons. First, the word 'atonement' has lost its meaning in ordinary English. It sounds strange and archaic. It causes people to react with blank stares or furrowed brows. Maybe the word meant something once upon a time. Now it just causes puzzlement. If we are to communicate the meaning of the cross, we simply cannot afford to use words which have lost their meaning for most people.

The second point concerns the use of the word 'theory'. It suggests a detailed, blow by blow account of everything we need to know about exactly how God redeems us through the cross of Christ. But the New Testament is not like this. It is not concerned with the detailed and intricate mechanics of redemption. The New Testament actually presents us with a series of images of what Christ achieved for us through his death and resurrection. It is dominated by proclamation of the *fact* that the cross and resurrection have the power to change us, along with a number of superb illustrations of the ways in which we can visualize this potential.

The New Testament is basically interested in six things:

1. It states that something *new* has come about through the cross and resurrection of Jesus Christ.

2. It declares that something objective has happened through the cross. The way in which God relates to us has been changed dramatically.

3. It affirms that the cross is able to change us completely.

4. It gives us helpful ways of thinking about the new relationship with God which results through the cross.

5. It tells us what we need to do in order to be changed by the cross.

6. It provides us with guidance about the new life and new lifestyle that result when we have been changed in this way.

The theologian can – and, I would suggest, ought to – try and think through the implications of what the New Testament is saying. And he or she will probably end up developing theories of the meaning of the cross. That is no bad thing, as part of our responsibility as Christians ought to be to think through the implications of our faith. But we need to appreciate that this process of reflection, although *based upon* the New Testament, actually *goes beyond* the New Testament. Theologians are perfectly at liberty to speak about 'theories of the atonement'. After all, every profession has its jargon; it becomes unhelpful, though, when they still use it in speaking to – or writing for – audiences which are, quite simply, baffled by what they say.

So for these reasons, I propose not to use the phrase 'theories of the atonement' at all; instead I am going to talk about 'images of salvation', ways of picturing and understanding what God achieved for us through the cross and resurrection of Christ.

4

The Cross in Images

I t was a brilliant Tuscan morning late one autumn in 1988. I had travelled to Florence to work on some unpublished fifteenth-century manuscripts. The manuscripts were held by one of the great Renaissance libraries in the city, whose history went back to the time of the Medicis. The library was set in a small courtyard, like a monastic cloister, with stone walkways, roofed with the brilliant red tiles for which Florence is famous, arranged around its four sides. It opened up on to a small garden. Plants grew in profusion within the garden, as they did over the masonry of the building itself.

I walked around the courtyard, waiting for the library to open. With all the enthusiasm of a scholar working abroad, I had turned up far too early. As I walked, I noticed that the garden took on completely different aspects. From one angle, it seemed to be dominated by roses. From another, citrus trees seemed to be growing everywhere. To appreciate it fully, I had to see it from every side. Each of the great arched glassless windows in the courtyard offered a different view of the same garden. Each view was like a snapshot, building up to give a composite picture of a greater whole.

The librarian arrived. I gathered my papers together, and prepared to start work for the day. My sense of anticipation was, however, rapidly flattened. She explained to me that, as it was a Monday, the library opened even later than usual. Dejected, I wandered off to a nearby square, and ordered a cup of coffee at one of its many pavement cafés. I consoled myself by reflecting that, as the manuscripts had been in the library for five hundred years, they could probably survive for another two hours. The square centred on the Duomo, Florence's great Renaissance cathedral. From my seat, I had a marvellous view of it – or, at least, of part of it. After finishing my coffee and consulting my watch, I spent the remainder of my time pottering round the cathedral, exploring its magnificent interior, and pretending I was Lucy Honeychurch in E. M. Forster's novel *A Room with a View*. Finally, I returned to the now open library, and immersed myself in my studies. After three days, I began to realize why the manuscripts remained unpublished after five hundred years – but that is another story.

But the events of that morning remained in my mind. It seemed that the bigger and more complicated something is, the more difficult it is to take it in at a single glance. The garden illustrated this point neatly, the cathedral more graphically. With any great building – like Notre Dame in Paris, the National Cathedral in Washington DC, or the Palace of Westminster in

London – you have to take time and effort to appreciate it. It is no good taking a quick look from the window of a passing coach or from a seat at a pavement café. You have to get out, and take the trouble to explore it from all kinds of angles and viewpoints. Otherwise its riches and wonders will remain largely hidden and undiscovered. It will have been 'seen' – but not understood or appreciated.

Those thoughts stayed in my mind for some time. As I walked to the library that Monday morning, I had been thinking about the enormous difficulty Christians have in doing justice to the cross of Christ. Our little theories about its meaning somehow seem terribly inadequate. I had been musing on the story told about Augustine of Hippo, the early Christian thinker who wrote an important work on the Trinity. He is rumoured to have been walking along the shore one day, presumably deep in thought, when he noticed a little boy pouring sea water into a hole in the sand. He scooped up water from the sea in his hands, and walked to the hole. After he had emptied his hands of the water, he returned to the sea once more. Augustine watched him for a few moments, then asked him what he was doing. 'I'm pouring the Mediterranean Sea into this hole in the ground,' was the reply. Augustine probably suppressed a smile. 'You're wasting your time! You can't do it! You'll never get the sea into that little hole in the ground.' To which the boy is meant to have replied, 'Well then you're wasting your time writing about God. You'll never get *him* into a book!'

The cross is like a great piece of architecture. Some approaches to it are like distant views of a cathedral, in which the whole building is seen. Others are like photographs of its towers and buttresses, or close-ups of its frescos, altarpieces or its crypt. They are all part of the same building, yet looking different and serving differing functions. Yet, like the different parts of a human body, they are all part of the same whole. They all have their distinct contributions to make. Remove some of them, and a false impression of the greater whole is created. The problem with many approaches to the cross is not so much that they are wrong, as that they are inadequate. Some people seem to think that one formula, sentence or analogy contains everything that needs to be said, or could ever be said, about the meaning of the cross of Christ. They supplement the understandable statement, 'This is all that I can make of the cross,' with the dogmatic assertion, 'and that is all that there is to it.' But there is always more to the cross than we can imagine. It is inexhaustible. We need to consider the collective witness of the church down the ages to the meaning of the cross. We cannot rely on the insights of a few individuals – or, still worse, our own views – as the best possible guide to the heart of the Christian faith. We need to listen to the conversations of others, who have wrestled with the same question before us. Maybe we can learn from them.

In this section, we shall be looking at five groups of images to be found in the New Testament. Three questions need to be asked about each image used by the New Testament writers to make sense of, and cast light upon, the mystery of the cross.

1. What does the image mean?

2. What does it tell us about our state apart from Christ?

3. How do we take hold of the benefits it offers us?

The third question is actually so important that it merits a chapter in itself; the present chapter will thus deal with the first two of these questions.

1. Images from a battlefield

'Thanks be to God! He gives us the victory through our Lord Jesus Christ' (1 Corinthians 15:57). These words present us with a simple and dignified explanation of the meaning of the cross and resurrection of Jesus Christ. The great reversal of Easter Day signals a victory. That victory might seem to belong exclusively to Christ and to be without relevance to us. But, as the full potential of Easter faith unfolded, it became clear that Christ's victory was charged with the power to transform the deadliness of mortal human life. Christ's victory can be our victory, through the grace of God.

But what sort of victory are we talking about? Is Easter Day just a reversal of the events of Good Friday? Are we to understand the resurrection simply as a divine counterattack, which restores the situation which previously existed? No. The New Testament theme of victory is not cheap triumphalism celebrating the temporary rout of a local invader. What, it must be asked in all honesty, would be so vitally important about one man being snatched from the clutches of death – when millions die daily, without any such hope?

Part of the answer to that question, as we saw earlier, lies in the realization of what it tells us about the identity of Jesus. But perhaps the greater part of that answer lies in a more thorough and painstaking exploration of the nature of the victory gained by Christ upon the cross. An analogy will bring out the point I have in mind.

Let us imagine a country in the most appalling distress. Let us pretend that it is located in Africa, and has been plagued by starvation and famine. Economic mismanagement has destroyed the country's ability to support itself. The western media bombard their public with images of this distress. A leading North American television network sends in a private jet, and evacuates a young man. It is presented as a gesture of support and sympathy. It is also surrounded by enormous publicity. The young man, we are told, will survive and prosper in the relative safety and prosperity of the West. He will be a symbol of hope for his people.

The action was brief, dramatic and newsworthy. But it utterly failed to change the situation back in Africa. All that happened was that a single person was extracted from the predicament of his people. No-one back home benefited. They just watched while he was removed to safety, while they were left to suffer, hopeless and helpless. In one sense, the removal of that young man from the situation was a symbol of abandonment, rather than of solidarity.

Meanwhile, unnoticed by the media publicity machines, the aid workers toil on in the background. They are not concerned with the cheap gimmicks of the publicity-hungry media. Their business is to address the deeply rooted problems of the African nation, which ultimately lie behind its current plight. Deforestation must be reversed, through a major programme of replanting. The nation's economy must be restructured. Its people must be given hope to face its problems, and the tools they need to rebuild its broken culture. The problems are just too deeply rooted and too far beneath the surface to be resolved in a single, quick, stroke. A long and difficult road lies ahead. Poverty and suffering will stalk this nation for many years to come. But the aid workers' commitment and dedication hold the key to this stricken nation's future. They will be there, unnoticed and unacknowledged by media attention, to guide and help the nation as it painfully and painstakingly rebuilds.

To talk unthinkingly about Jesus' victory over death can often come dangerously close to that first approach, in all its glorious superficiality and shallowness. It is good news for one person; the rest of us are, however, left stranded in our situation. Yet I cannot stress sufficiently that the New Testament does not see the resurrection in this light. Rather, it interprets the resurrection as a token and pledge of God's total commitment to the making right of his creation. God is like the aid workers who were committed to the rebuilding of a nation, despite the enormous problems they faced. The resurrection is seen as a glorious and powerful symbol of the purpose and power of God to deal with the real problems of the human predicament. It tells us that God is willing and able to put right the real disorders of our broken existence. It declares that God is confronting the root causes of human misery and pain.

But the resurrection is no mere symbol. *It really happened.* The resurrection is perhaps the most powerful, exciting and *noticeable* aspect of the entire history of salvation. But we must not think that God's decision to redeem us somehow starts with that resurrection. Rather, it should be seen as a spectacular climax to the long process of restoring wayward humanity. That process begins in history with Abraham and the people of Israel, and continues in our own day and age. The resurrection of Jesus is a sign of God's purpose and power to restore his creation to its full stature and integrity. Just as death could be seen as the culmination of all that is wrong with the world, so the resurrection can be seen as a pledge of God's ultimate victory over the disorder which plagues his creation on account of the fall. Death is the greatest enemy, and yet death has been defeated by God through Christ. And so we are given hope that the remainder of the powers and forces that confront us are similarly being defeated and their power broken.

The cross spells freedom. It brings liberation from *false understandings of God*. It shows that God is *there* – despite all the suggestions that he is not. Good Friday seemed to confirm the idea that God was dead, asleep or indifferent. Easter Day showed that God was alive, well and caring. The cross frees us from the idea that human nature is somehow too sinful, or the human dilemma too complex, for God to do anything about it. The surly bonds which tie us to these deeply pessimistic and oppressive views of God are torn apart by the cross. God is shown as one who is passionately committed to the well-being and salvation of his creation – so much so, in fact, that he is prepared to enter into that creation, and redeem it from within. The creator becomes a creature within his own creation, in order to recreate it. In the aftermath of Gethsemane, we catch the fragrance of Eden. Jesus was betrayed within the garden of Gethsemane, in order to undo the disobedience of human nature within the garden of Eden. The resurrection is like the first day of a new creation.

So how does this image of what God achieved through the cross help us make sense of sin? What does it tell us about our situation apart from Christ? It encourages us to think of sin as enslavement and oppression. That enslavement could be political, military or economic. It is like the oppression which burdened the Israelites in Egypt, and which so grievously affects many people in poorer nations today. It invites us to imagine the sense of despair and hopelessness which plagued the continent of Europe in the darker days of Nazi occupation. It declares, '*This* is what sin is like.' It reminds us that an objective state of oppression leads to a subjective feeling of oppression. No amount of tinkering around with the subjective side of things can ever change the real situation, which causes that sense of despair in the first place. Real peace of mind requires a real change in our situation.

Sin is like a force, which hold us in captivity. It is disruptive. It draws us away from God, and submerges us in sin. We cannot control this situation. It is like being taken captive by a strong man: the only way in which we can be set free is through someone stronger overwhelming him, and allowing us to escape. Think of the cross and resurrection of Jesus as breaking the power of sin.

But if the power of sin, death and evil has been broken, how can we make sense of the fact that it still continues to plague us? Human history and Christian experience tell us of a constant struggle against sin and evil in our own lives, even as Christians. There is a real danger, it would seem, that talking about 'the victory of faith' will become nothing more than empty words, masking a contradiction between faith and experience. How can we handle this problem?

A helpful way of understanding this difficulty was developed by a group of distinguished writers, such as C. S. Lewis in England and Anders Nygren in Sweden. They noticed important parallels between the New Testament and the situation during the Second World War. The victory won over sin through the death of Christ was like the liberation of an occupied country from Nazi rule. We need to allow our imaginations to take in the sinister and menacing idea of an occupying power. Life has to be lived under the shadow of this foreign presence. And part of the poignancy of the situation is its utter hopelessness. Nothing can be done about it. No-one can defeat it.

Then comes the electrifying news. There has been a far-off battle. And somehow, it has turned the tide of the war. A new phase has developed, and the occupying power is in disarray. Its backbone has been broken. In the course of time, the Nazis will be driven out of every corner of Europe. But they are still present in the occupied country.

In one sense, the situation has not changed, but in another, more important, sense, the situation has changed totally. The scent of victory and liberation is in the air. A total change in the psychological climate results. I remember once meeting a man who had been held prisoner in a Japanese prisoner-of-war camp in Singapore. He told me of the astonishing change in the camp atmosphere which came about when one of the prisoners (who owned a shortwave radio) learned of the collapse of the Japanese war effort in the middle of 1945. Although all in the camp still remained prisoners, they knew that their enemy had been beaten. It would only be a matter of time before they were released. And those prisoners, I was told, began to laugh and cry, as if they were free already.

The end of the Second World War in Europe came about a year after the establishment of the bridgeheads in Normandy in June 1944. But an objective change had taken place some time before in the theatre of war – with a resulting subjective change in the hearts and minds of captive people. And so with us now. In one sense, victory has not come; in another, it has. The resurrection declares in advance of the event God's total victory over all evil and oppressive forces – such as death, evil and sin. Their backbone has been broken, and we may begin to live *now* in the light of that victory, knowing that the long night of their oppression will end.

2. Images from a court of law

One of the major themes which resounds throughout the Christian discussion of redemption is that of the justice and righteousness of God. God does not redeem us in some arbitrary and haphazard manner, but in a way which both accords with and declares his righteousness.[24] It is therefore natural that the imagery and language of the lawcourt should be part of the Christian way of speaking about the meaning of the cross.

Perhaps one of the most important aspects of this way of approaching the cross relates to sin. Sin can be understood in legal, or penal, terms. It is an offence against God. This must not be confused with the idea of some petty insult, as if sin was like being rude to someone. Sin amounts to a violation of the moral ordering of the creation, established by God himself at the foundation of the world. Sin is an offence against the moral fabric of the creation, not just some personal insult to God.

An analogy may make this point clearer. If I were to kidnap someone, and hold them to ransom, I would be guilty of a personal offence against that individual. But I would also be guilty of something greater – an offence against society as a whole, which rightly wants to discourage people from behaving in this way. Private morality and public law cannot be separated in this case. Similarly, sin is not a private matter. It has to be dealt with publicly. It threatens to break down the moral ordering of the creation, upon which its continued well-being depends.

So how can God forgive human sin, without himself violating that moral order? Why can't God just forgive sin, and have done with it? Why not just declare that all sin – past, present and future – is cancelled and forgiven? Because this would be to deny the seriousness of sin. It would be to fail to safeguard creation against corruption and contamination. It would be to make a mockery of the idea of justice, pretending that sin is just some private matter, of no public relevance.

Sin causes an offence, and that offence must be dealt with. In personal relationships it is, sadly, common for offence to be given to someone. And when that happens, it is pointless pretending that no offence was given. That is to live in a world which bears no relation to the harsh realities of human life. When offence is given, it must be confronted and healed (a point we shall explore further in dealing with the image of personal relationships).

It is here that the cross becomes of central importance. It condemns sin, showing up its full seriousness. Sin, which might seem to be a trivial matter, leads to the state of affairs where God himself ends up by being crucified. So perverted and confused has the moral ordering of the creation become on account of human sin that the creation ends up attempting to destroy its creator. Something radical has to be done to restore the harmony of the world, to cancel its guilt in order that it may start again, and break the power of the disruptive forces within it. Yet so deeply is the creation, and supremely human nature, enmeshed in sin, that it cannot get itself out of its accumulation of sin, guilt and inherited punishment. Like a bad debt, it keeps getting bigger, with no hope of any way of clearing the decks, and starting all over again. Action from outside is required, if we are to break free from this self-imposed prison.

The cross marks a turning point in this situation. The enmity with God is ended by the cross. God's relation to us changes – and thus enables our relationship with him to change. The barrier which sin posed to our friendship with God is broken down by Christ. The temple curtain at Jerusalem was often seen as a symbol of the inability of ordinary people to enter into the presence of God. This curtain was torn at the time of Christ's death.[25] This itself is a powerful symbol of the way in which the death of Christ broke down the barrier of sin. The way has been opened for us to return to God.

In the incarnation, God has taken upon himself the burden of human guilt. Christ is the one who bore the weight of human sin upon his lonely and exhausted shoulders at Calvary.[26] 'God made him who had no sin to be sin for us' (2 Corinthians 5:21). Christ was content to be reckoned among sinners, in order to redeem sinners.[27] 'He himself bore our sins in his body on the tree, so that we might die to sin and live for righteousness; by his wounds you have been healed' (1 Peter 2:24). The cross brings home both the seriousness of sin, and the power and purpose of God to engage with it, eventually to destroy it. In the cross we see real forgiveness of real sins – our sins. The initiative is from God – the response must be from us. God moves, so that we can move. God loved us, in order that we might love him.[28]

God thus does what only he could do. He takes away both the guilt and the power of human sin. He was under no obligation to do so. But in his mercy and compassion, he chose to act in this way. At no point is his righteousness compromised. Such is his love for us that he takes upon himself the pain and suffering which, by rights, should have been ours. As Paul once wrote, 'I live by faith in the Son of God, who loved me and gave himself for me' (Galatians 2:20). In the end, we can never give a full account of how this astonishing change takes place. It is something that should make us get down on our knees in adoration and praise, rather than cause us to speculate endlessly on what was going on behind the theological scenes. The best theologians have always been those who worship and adore the crucified Christ, rather than those who try to reduce him to neat theories.

However, to think theologically is human, and it is important for us to bring our rational mind, as well as faith, to bear on this issue. So here, briefly stated, are the three main ways of trying to understand how the cross enables us to be forgiven.

a. *Representation*. Christ is here understood to be the covenant representative of humanity. Through faith, we are part of the covenant between God and humanity. All that Christ has won for us through the cross is available to us, on account of the covenant. Just as God entered into a covenant with his people Israel, so he has entered into a covenant with his church. Christ, by his obedience upon the cross, represents his covenant people, winning benefits for them as their representative – including the full and free forgiveness of our sins.

b. *Participation*. Through faith, believers are 'in Christ', to use Paul's famous phrase. They are caught up in him, and share in his risen life. As a result of this, they share in all the benefits won by Christ, through his obedience upon the cross. One of those benefits is the forgiveness of sins, in which we share through our faith. Participating in Christ thus entails the forgiveness of our sins, and sharing in his righteousness.

c. *Substitution*. Christ is here understood to be our substitute, the one who goes to the cross in our place. There is no limit to the extent to which Christ is prepared to identify with us. We deserved punishment, on account of our sins. God allows Christ to stand in our place, taking our guilt upon himself, so that his righteousness – won by obedience upon the cross – might become ours. Christ enters into our human situation, sharing its sorrows, its pain and its guilt. And all these are brought to the cross. They are nailed to that cross, along with the one who bears them for us. And by his wounds, we are healed.

Each of these three approaches casts priceless light on how we come to benefit from the death and resurrection of Christ, and how our guilt comes to be replaced by his righteousness. We shall further develop the idea of sharing in Christ's person and his benefits in the chapter which follows. For the moment, however, our attention shifts to another way of thinking about the cross and resurrection which is set in a legal context – justification.

Christ 'was delivered over to death for our sins and was raised to life for our justification' (Romans 4:25). The term 'justification', which is a particular favourite with Paul, has its origins in the Hebrew lawcourts. It refers primarily – but not exclusively – to an action in a lawcourt by which a judge decides in favour of one party, rather than the other. The individual who is justified is the one who has been declared to be in the right in the sight of the court. The term is notoriously difficult to render in English, on account of the richness of its associations in Hebrew.[29] Think about ideas like 'being put in the right', 'being declared to be in the right', 'restored' or 'vindicated'. These go some way towards indicating the richness of this way of thinking about what God has achieved for and in us through Jesus Christ. It is, however, the *fact* of justification (rather than a specific doctrine of justification) which dominates the New Testament. The New Testament writers (especially Paul and James) are perhaps more concerned to explore the consequences of justification, rather than its preconditions.

But our concern here is to cast light on the cross and resurrection of Jesus Christ. How are we to make sense of the scriptural idea of justification, when the word itself is rather unusual in modern English? Isn't there a danger that justification, like atonement, will become little more than a piece of religious jargon, restricted to the Christian ghetto, and having no real meaning outside the Christian situation? And won't this cause all sorts of difficulties in communicating the gospel? After all, Paul uses the word 'justification' extensively to explain the meaning of the cross and resurrection. Yet this word is not used much outside Christian circles. As a result, we have a formidable communication problem on our hands! What does 'justification' mean in today's everyday world? It could mean a defence of one's position in an argument or legal case. Or it might be the process of making right-hand margins uniform down a printed page. So how can a term most familiar from the world of arguments or wordprocessing have any real relevance for Christian attempts to make sense of the cross?

The basic idea here is that of 'making right'. The English word 'justification' is an attempt to denote the Old Testament idea of being 'right before God'. To have faith is to be right with God – that is, to live in an attitude of trust in God. Faith is the right way to live, in the sight of God. It may therefore be helpful if the word 'justification' is paraphrased, perhaps to give 'being right with God'. Similarly, 'to be justified' could be paraphrased as 'to be put in a right relationship with God'.

However, the phrase 'justification by faith' can easily be misunderstood to mean that we are justified *on account of faith*. In other words, the human activity of faith is the basis of God's decision to grant us the status of being righteous in his sight. If this were the case, this would amount to a doctrine of justification by works, with faith merely being seen as a special type of good work.

In fact, the phrase 'justification by faith' has a quite different meaning. It is because of Jesus Christ, and not because of anything we have done or will do, that we are made right with God. But the means by which we are justified is faith. Faith is like a channel, through which the benefits of Christ flow to us. Faith is the means by which the work of Christ is applied to our lives. This is no doctrine of justification on account of human achievement. It is a doctrine of justification on account of what Christ achieved for us.

But the doctrine of 'justification by faith' implies still more than this. The very faith through which we are justified is itself a gift of God. Faith is not something which we can achieve; it is something achieved within us by God. Everything necessary for salvation has been done, and done well, by God. Faith is God's work within us, the God-given channel by which the 'benefits of Christ' can be conveyed to believers. Perhaps the more lengthy phrase 'justification by grace through faith' makes this point more clearly.

The doctrine of justification by faith does not devalue or discourage human ethical action. The doctrine tells us that we are not justified on account of our moral activities. We don't find acceptance in the sight of God by doing good things. It is because we are accepted by God that we long to do good. So good works are an entirely appropriate and natural response to our justification. They are the result, not the cause, of justification. Martin Luther uses the image of a fruit tree to make this point. Justification represents God's gracious establishment of a good root system (faith), on account of which fruit (good works) will naturally follow. The doctrine liberates us from the oppressive mindset which declares that we must be high achievers before we can enter the kingdom of God. But in no way does it discourage us from becoming high achievers for God after our justification.

Despite the unfamiliarity of the idea, justification has an invaluable potential to convey certain key elements of the 'word of the cross'. Suppose we choose to interpret justification as 'putting right', perhaps translating the term as *rectification*. What does this imply? This potent idea conveys the notion of a disruption within the nature of things, including human nature itself. It represents an awareness of the deep-rooted *wrongness* of things as they now stand – a state of affairs which is seen at its worst in the crucifixion itself. How mixed up the world has become, how far it has departed from its maker's intentions, that when God chose to visit and redeem his people,[30] that very same people chose to crucify him. There are few more powerful and telling indictments of the ways things are than this. Sin is both personal and structural. It reflects the way in which individuals and societies have become so fractured, disintegrated and corrupted that people can no longer live happily and effectively. To speak of God's transformation of the situation as justification is to describe the problem in terms of disruption and disintegration. The way things are isn't the way things are meant to be. Someone has to begin the task of putting our fragmented and broken world back together again – morally and spiritually. The doctrine of justification tells us that God is doing just that. The resurrection is like the first day of a new creation, in which the work and world of the old Adam are being taken to bits and put back together again. And all on account of the radical and creative obedience of the new Adam, Jesus Christ.

The difficulties we've noted in making sense of the term 'justification' make especially obvious a problem that we have with many other terms whose meaning we take for granted. Just because a word is familiar to our hearers doesn't mean they understand it. For example, the word 'salvation' is familiar – but it needs explaining, if its real Christian meaning is to come across. C. S. Lewis once wrote:

> We must learn the language of our audience. And let me say at the outset that it is no use laying down *a priori* what the 'plain man' does or does not understand. You have to find out by experience . . . You must translate every bit of your theology into the vernacular. This is very troublesome . . . but it is essential. It is also of the greatest service to your own thought. I have come to the conclusion that if you cannot translate your own thoughts into

uneducated language, then your thoughts are
confused. Power to translate is the test of
having really understood your own
meaning.[31]

Perhaps there is a good case to be made for forcing
us to think through all the terms of our Christian
vocabulary, and making sure that we could explain
them to a non-Christian audience. One of our greatest
failings as Christians is that we bandy about words
such as 'salvation', 'redemption' and 'grace'. But we
rarely take the trouble to make sure that they make
sense to the people we're talking to. And do we really
understand them ourselves?

The second legal image we shall consider is much
easier to handle – adoption. Through what Christ
achieved for us on the cross, we are adopted as the
children of God (Romans 8:23; 9:4; Ephesians 1:5).
The legal significance of the idea is simple. Individuals
who are born outside a family are given the legal status
of belonging to that family on adoption. To be
adopted is to receive a radical change in one's legal
status. A poor child adopted by a rich family comes to
share in all the status and wealth of that household. To
be adopted is to receive the same inheritance rights as
the natural children.

The importance of this way of thinking about the
meaning of the cross can be seen by following through
Paul's argument in Romans 8:15–17. We could para-
phrase the argument like this. Consider the marvellous
sequence of events which leads from Calvary through
the resurrection to the giving of the Spirit at Pentecost.
On account of these events, believers are adopted, and
given the status of being children of God. If Jesus
Christ is the Son of God by nature, then we are the

children of God by adoption. But we are all the same children of God, whether that status is established by nature or by law. And that means that we all have the same inheritance rights. We are thus 'heirs of God, and co-heirs with Christ' (Romans 8:17).

So what are those rights? And how can we be reassured that we share in them? Paul points to what happened to Jesus Christ as a model of what will happen to us. What God bequeathed to Jesus Christ, his natural Son, he will bequeath to us, who share in those inheritance rights by faith. And that inheritance is suffering and glory. Just as Christ's sufferings at Calvary led to his glorification, so we must share in the same suffering before we can be glorified. Paul here rules out a cheap route to glory: glory comes only through suffering. But his overall point is positive: those who are suffering with Christ are those who will one day be glorified with Christ, entering into the same inheritance. So suffering is not a sign of spiritual shame or disgrace. Rather, it is a sign of sharing in the inheritance of faith. 'We share in his sufferings in order that we may also share in his glory' (Romans 8:17).

How should we think of our status apart from Christ? What images of sin do these ways of thinking about the cross and resurrection suggest? One basic idea comes across very powerfully here. It is that of *a wrong legal status in the sight of God*. Sin has legal aspects. It can be thought of as moral guilt, which is cancelled through the death of Christ. It can be seen as a verdict of 'guilty', pronounced by God on account of our sin. It can be thought of as 'being wrong with God', which is changed into 'being right with God' through the cross. It can be thought of as having no inheritance rights. By the grace of God, this situation and our status are changed beyond recognition through Christ's achievement at Calvary.

Finally, a misunderstanding needs to be noted. Some writers have spoken of such ways of making sense of the cross as being a 'legal fiction'. God treats us as if we are something that we are not – and by doing so, deceives himself and the world. How can God treat us as if we are righteous, when in fact we are sinful? This is something which cannot be tolerated. It is a legal fiction. But this rests on a misunderstanding. To explore this, let us consider a related topic.

Many of the Old Testament books make use of what is called 'the prophetic perfect'. As the prophet looks ahead to his vision of what God is going to do for his people, his language begins to change. That which actually lies in the future is transferred to the present. Yet the prophet sees that future action as already accomplished. God has promised to do it – and so it may be treated as if it has already been done. The faithfulness of God to his promises underlies this visionary sense of the future breaking into the present.

Legal images of salvation rest on a similar vision of God's redeeming activity. God has promised to redeem us through the work of Christ. He has promised to take sinners and redeem them from the penalty, the power and the presence of sin. That vision of redemption lies in the future, in that it is not totally accomplished at this moment. But the faithful promise of God is there, and it is for real. The present reality of sin is to be seen in the light of the vision of redeemed humanity, made perfect through all that Christ achieved on the cross.

And the wonderful thing is this. Though we are sinners now, we can rest assured that this vision will be realized – faithfully and totally. And we may rejoice now in that knowledge. We may take heart from knowing that the sinner we now know will one day give way to the righteous person in Christ. God does not treat us as if we were righteous; he declares that we will be righteous, and that we can rest assured of that fact now. The sinner, who one day will be righteous, can rejoice in that hope, just as the sick person, who will one day be cured, can take comfort from that assurance. This is no fiction: it is a faithful promise by a God who has shown his faithfulness by sending his Son to die for us.

3. Images from a rehabilitation clinic

A third set of images derives from the field of personal relationships, and is used throughout the New Testament, and especially in the parables of Jesus. Personal relationships can give us insights into our relationship with God, and the way in which this is transformed by the cross. Two such images are of especial importance.

The first is Paul's idea of 'reconciliation'. Through Christ, God was reconciling the world to himself (2 Corinthians 5:19). The idea of reconciliation would have been well known to Paul's readers, as it is today. Reconciliation means bringing back together two people who have suffered a breakdown in their relationship. Paul uses the word elsewhere in this sense, when he speaks of the reconciliation of a husband and wife who have become separated (1 Corinthians 7:11). As a result, the relationship is healed. It is restored and renewed. The cross offers us reconciliation. It offers to restore and renew our broken personal relationship with God. The cross thus criticizes and affirms us at one and the same time. It criticizes us, in that it tell us we aren't right with God. But it affirms us, in that it shows the remarkable extent to which God is prepared to go, in order to bring us back to him. We must matter a lot to him, if he is prepared to go through the torment of Calvary to bring us home.

The second image is that of forgiveness. Forgiveness is essential if a broken relationship is to be fully restored. Where offence has been given and wounds have been inflicted, it is essential that this hurt and pain should be acknowledged and confronted, if restoration is to come about. Forgiveness comes about only when the offended person is able to explain to the offender the full hurt that has been caused, and the pain that has been inflicted. It requires a painful initiative to be taken – confronting the offender, in order that all the pain and hurt can be admitted and resolved. That is the initiative that God undertook in sending Jesus Christ to die upon the cross.

For the cross reveals the full extent of the love of God for us. The full measure of that love can be seen by reflecting on everything that Jesus Christ endured at Calvary – and realizing that this was *for us*. God's love is seen in action on Calvary. He brings home to us, at one and the same time, how much we matter to him – and how much we have sinned against him. The offer of forgiveness made through the cross is painful to accept. It means realizing that the pain and suffering of Calvary somehow came about on account of our sin. But we are being offered *real* forgiveness of *real* sins, not the cloud–cuckoo–land kind of forgiveness that results from papering over cracks. The problems are resolved, not ignored. The cross faces up to the real issues. And the relationship is transformed through our joyful tears of human repentance and divine for- giveness. It may be painful – but it's the real thing.

The image also brings home to us the shallowness of

those who say, 'Why bother to do anything? God has forgiven your sin, and that's the end of it. You can just relax.' This shockingly superficial approach would be unacceptable even in human relationships, let alone our relationship with God. For it suggests that no response is necessary to an offer of forgiveness. It ignores our need to say 'Yes!' to God's offer of forgiveness. It overlooks the transforming power of the joyful acceptance of pardon. For a relationship to be reconstructed, both its parties must be willing for it to be transformed. Forgiveness offered, and not accepted, is powerless to transform. The offer of forgiveness that is lovingly made to us through the cross of Christ demands a response from us. But consider the tender and loving kindness of the God who humbles himself to make that offer. It's hard to say 'no' to that kind of love.

This way of approaching the meaning of the cross also allows us to appreciate the importance of another key theme. A central aspect of Jesus' ministry is the acceptance of those reckoned unacceptable by society. Time and time again, Jesus sits at table with or ministers to people who are social outcasts.[32] Here is no abstract theorizing about personal or social relationships. Jesus sets about relating to people, instead of merely talking about it. He is able and willing to associate with those who are deemed to be excluded from relationships by everyone else. If God is prepared to relate to us, sinners though we are, we ought to be prepared to relate to those whom we instinctively regard as outcasts. Just as God values us, despite our sin, so we must learn to value others. The love of God has grasped us, even if we have yet to grasp it fully.

This point about being *valued* by God needs further exploration. My wife works in an Oxford rehabilitation unit. It specializes in dealing with people who have suffered head injuries. The effect that these injuries have on people can be catastrophic. The unit cares for people now confined to wheelchairs and needing permanent care. These are people who were once capable of looking after themselves and living life to the full. All that was changed by head injuries. And sadly, brain damage rarely heals. Relatives, shocked by the change they see, often ask a devastating question, 'When will they get better?' And the dreadful answer is that they probably will never recover. Part of the tragedy for the relatives is that they knew the people who are now so powerless and helpless when they were fit and able. A pathetic sense of sadness is evoked by the image of these patients. Their worlds have been shattered by their injuries.

Here, then, is an image of brokenness, of lives that have been shattered, and of hopes that have been dashed. Yet despite the fact that these patients have been written off as useless by the world, they are still valued and loved by the staff at the rehabilitation centre. They take time and trouble over them, rejoicing in the slightest sign of improvement. There is a quality of commitment here, absent from the world at large. Here is a community within which these people are valued and esteemed. The world regards them as worthless; yet here, they are precious. And even though we, as sinners, are broken and worthless, the cross declares to us the amazing fact that we *matter*. We matter profoundly to God, despite the fact that there is nothing about us which merits such care, concern and compassion. God's love for us may well reflect his kindness and generosity, rather than our own intrinsic worth – but that is not the point. God loved us so much that Christ died for us.[33]

The cross brings home to us the amazing extent of the love of God for broken human beings like us. God values those whom the world writes off as being devoid of value. God takes trouble over those whom the world regards as scarcely worth bothering about. And God saves those whom the world regards as weak and foolish. The gospel invites us to rejoice in the fact that God values and affirms us, despite all our failings and shortcomings. But it does more than that. It asks us to extend that same calibre and quality of affirming love to those whom the world regards as devoid of value. For isn't this how the love of God is made known in the dark corners of this world?

What do these images of transformed personal and social relationships tell us about our state apart from Christ? If we need to be forgiven by and reconciled to God through the death of Christ on the cross, what does this tell us about our present situation? The offer of reconciliation points to a real need on our part. It tells us that we are alienated from God. It tells us that we are far from him, in much the same way as the prodigal son wandered far from his father. It tells us that our relationship with God falls far short of what it is intended to be, and what it can be. We may be children of God in name – but in reality, we are alienated children of God. We are not born into the fulness of our relationship with God; that has to be established. Our natural state is that of alienation from the God who created us – and who offers to redeem us.

Let us return to the image of the patients, for it allows us insights into the way God must feel about his creation. The patients' relatives were saddened by their state. They might have been healthy and prosperous, but now they are broken and helpless. Might not God feel the same about his child of creation? The innocence of Eden is transformed into the betrayal of Gethsemane. That which God created good and healthy has become disabled, fractured, frail and infirm. The sheer tragedy of this situation can only be appreciated by comparing the way things are – the way *we* are – with the glorious way things were meant to be.

The Christian tradition has long used a helpful image to express this sense of estrangement and decay. The image of 'the fall' tries to bring together a range of biblical ideas relating to our predicament. It attempts to convey the sense of misery and tragedy which inevitably arises when we reflect on our situation. The crucifixion of Jesus just shows us how far we have fallen. We would like to think that, should God choose to visit his creation, we would welcome him with open arms, and lay on a reception for him. If governments put on such banquets for visiting heads of state, surely we would do the same for God. If that is the ideal, the reality is sadly different. When God visited his world, he was taken captive and killed by his own people. That simple reflection brings home to us how fallen human nature is – and how much it stands in need of restoration. And it opens up illuminating insights on how the cross relates to our needs.

4. Images from a prison

There are few more powerful images of despair than those which centre upon captivity. Joseph's imprisonment in Egypt; Israel's captivity in Egypt; Jerusalem's exile in Babylon: all evoke a tragic sense of despair at one's situation, linked with a wistful longing for freedom. The sense of being shaped and governed by unseen malign forces came to be a powerful and illuminating way of thinking about human sin. Israel's political domination by foreign powers such as Egypt or Babylon is one example. Another is the way in which individuals around Galilee were possessed by demons at the time of Jesus. Sin was like a power, a hidden force, capable of exerting an oppressive influence over our lives. And this sense of powerlessness was made unbearable by the knowledge that nothing could be done about it.

Such images evoked a powerful sense of the futility of the human situation. The theme of the powerlessness of humans to change their own situation resonates throughout the Old Testament, which stresses the need to look to the Lord for redemption, deliverance and renewal. The cross and resurrection of Jesus Christ are seen as representing precisely these long-awaited and long-hoped-for acts of deliverance.

So how is this act of deliverance to be understood? The New Testament draws upon and extends the long catalogue of divine acts of deliverance which we find in the Old Testament. God acted to deliver his people from servitude in Egypt. He acted to bring his people home from exile in Babylon. And now, he acts again – through the cross and resurrection of Jesus Christ. In one sense, the same pattern of release from bondage repeats itself. Slaves in the American deep south during the nineteenth century found enormous consolation and hope in reflecting on the exodus story. One day, they too might be delivered from slavery. Yet in another sense, a vital new development can be discerned. For the cross and resurrection of Jesus liberate us from a network of enslaving forces which penetrate right to the heart of the human predicament.

In delivering Israel from captivity in Egypt, God set

73

her free from a very specific set of oppressive forces. Not everyone is in bondage in Egypt today. The exodus from Egypt could be seen as a model[34] for liberation from other oppressive situations (such as slavery in the American deep south, or poverty in Latin America). But it must not make us think of our redemption in purely political and social terms. While these are key elements of any responsible Christian understanding of salvation, it must be stressed that there is more to real redemption than political liberation.

The cross and resurrection address additional, deeper problems of the human situation. They go beyond the specific situations of Egypt or Babylon. They identify a set of more fundamental forces which gave rise to those situations in the first place. These are forces such as the human thirst for power and a desire to break away from God. They could also include a reluctance to put one's trust fully in God, and the pervasive human fear of death. These are not restricted to any specific historical situation. These are perennial features of fallen human nature.

On a naive understanding of human nature, one might expect that, once Israel had been delivered from Egypt and had settled in the promised land, all would be sweetness and light. A golden age would dawn in the history of the people of Israel. Not a bit of it. As the Old Testament prophets, especially Amos and Hosea, made abundantly clear, Israel soon lapsed into comfortable self-centred ways, losing sight of her responsibilities towards God. Israel may have been liberated, at least for a while, from foreign oppression – but she soon fell captive to other forces. As Amos in particular makes clear, sin is not just something that affects those outside Israel; it perennially affects the people of God.

And so a central question begins to form in our minds. Is there any way in which we could be liberated from these fundamental forces, which collectively hold us captive? Can we escape from the stranglehold of sin, which prevents us from fully realizing the glorious freedom of the children of God? In the past, God may have acted to free Israel from captivity in some distant country, far, far away, and long, long ago. But what about us, here and now?

The New Testament affirms that the cross and resurrection demonstrate the ability and the intention of God to liberate us from the domination of sin. It uses a series of powerful and evocative images to explore this aspect of the cross. Two are of especial importance – 'ransom' and 'redemption'. We shall explore these individually.

Mark's gospel is one of the most moving pieces of literature ever to have been written. In part, its effectiveness arises from the tender way in which Mark portrays the frailty of the disciples. Here, Mark seems to be saying, were people who stood alongside Jesus at every major moment in his public ministry – and yet they *still* have difficulty in understanding him! Yet Mark does not condemn the disciples. It is almost as if he is hinting that they are typical of the rest of us – slow to understand the mysterious ways of God, and reluctant to have the familiarity of their old ways challenged. Perhaps the clearest instance of this concerns Jesus' prediction of his suffering and death on the cross.[35] Probably convinced that the messiah was to be a victorious and triumphant conquering hero, the disciples find they cannot cope with the idea of Jesus suffering and dying. Why should that happen? What purpose would it serve?

Maybe Jesus anticipated these unspoken questions

when he declared, 'the Son of Man did not come to be served, but to serve, and to give his life as a ransom for many' (Mark 10:45).[36] What ideas do these words suggest? What trains of thought would be set off by this image of 'ransom'? Three come to mind immediately.

a. *Liberation.* A ransom is something which achieves freedom for a person who is held in captivity. When someone is kidnapped, and a ransom demanded, the payment of that ransom leads to liberation. To speak of Jesus' death as a ransom is thus to point to the setting free of captives, to the liberation of people, and to the ending of a period of imprisonment. We have been set free from captivity to sin and the fear of death (Romans 8:2; Hebrews 2:15).

b. *Payment.* A ransom is a sum of money which is paid in order to achieve an individual's liberation. The more important the person who is held captive, the greater the price which has to be paid.[37] The New Testament declares that the death of Christ is the price of our liberation.[38] This brings home to us the costliness of our redemption. The Son of God died in order that we might be set free, and achieve life in all its fulness and freedom.

c. *Someone to whom the ransom is paid.* A ransom is usually paid to an individual's captor, or his agent. But there is not a hint in the New Testament that Jesus' death was the price paid to someone (such as the devil) to achieve our liberation. Some of the writers of the first four centuries, however, assumed that they could press this analogy right to its limits. They declared that God had delivered us from the power of the devil by

76

offering Jesus to him as the price of our liberation. This idea, however, is without scriptural foundation. It amounts to a serious distortion of the New Testament understanding of the meaning of the death of Jesus Christ. The analogy had been forced to its limits, and had broken down. Yet there was nothing wrong with the analogy. The problem lay with those who wanted to base themselves on Scripture, and yet to go beyond what Scripture tells us.

It is therefore important to consider how far we are allowed to press analogies before they break down and mislead us. The analogy of ransom is profoundly helpful, when used responsibly. But if it is pressed too far, it becomes misleading. So how do we know when we are pressing an analogy too far? Happily, this difficulty is nothing like as great as it might seem at first sight. There are many scriptural analogies of redemption, all of which combine to build up a reliable picture of all that has been done for us through Christ. And these analogies interact. They qualify one another, and allow each to be interpreted properly. Press any one of them too far, and we pass outside the common core of conviction that all of them express. The same point is evident from the second image we shall consider – redemption.

Redemption is a word that many Christians use happily – and thoughtlessly. What does the word actually mean? The Greek word that lies behind the term could be translated along the following lines: 'to remove from the marketplace'. This is not especially helpful or illuminating, unless you happen to be aware of the specific setting which this image envisages. That context is the liberation of a slave, who is thus 'removed from the marketplace'. He is no longer treated as a commodity. He is instead granted the dignity of personhood which accompanies freedom. The image of redemption thus immediately suggests the joy of freedom and the achievement of personal dignity which come with emancipation from slavery. To be redeemed is to be treated as a person, not an object. It is to become a citizen of heaven, rather than a slave of the earth.

Slaves, however, were important merchandise in the ancient world. And someone had to foot the bill for their liberation (which explains why it was a relatively unusual, but far from totally unknown, event). The image of redemption thus points also to the need for payment. Redemption is costly. The better a slave, the greater the payment required for redemption, on account of the greater resulting loss to the owner. When it uses the image of redemption to make sense of the cross, the New Testament is at one and the same time stressing two things. In the first place, it emphasizes the costliness of redemption. The Son of God had to die in order that we might be redeemed. In the second, it underscores the generosity of God in undertaking to purchase our liberty at his expense. God foots the bill of our redemption, and offers us our freedom and dignity as a gift.

But is there a slave-owner to whom a price is paid? From whom are we redeemed? The New Testament is silent. The analogy has broken down. To press it further is to run the risk of distortion and misunderstanding. Responsible theology learns that there are limits placed upon its speculation. There is much theological wisdom in the old saying, 'Fools rush in where angels fear to tread.'

Finally, let us consider the imagery of the prison a little longer. What sort of impressions or associations does it bring to mind? The following might flash through our minds. It could mean being confined in a dark cell, cut off from the world outside. This isolation leads to hopelessness and despair. It might mean being tied up, or bound with chains and manacles. In short, it is an image of loneliness, helplessness and hopelessness. But all this is changed by the gospel. The prison door of our lives is thrown open, and we are invited to walk, as free men and women, into the light of day. Charles Wesley puts this memorably in his famous hymn 'And can it be?', which forms a fitting end to our reflections on this theme:

> Long my imprisoned spirit lay
>   Fast bound in sin and nature's night;
> Thine eye diffused a quickening ray,—
>   I woke, the dungeon flamed with light;
> My chains fell off, my heart was free,
> I rose, went forth, and followed thee.

5. Images from a hospital

In Scripture, healing is often used as an image of salvation. In other words, the process of restoring someone to health is an analogy for what Christ achieves for us through his cross and resurrection. Jesus' healing miracles are not seen as an arbitrary or pointless demonstration of power, as if he were some kind of spiritual showman. Instead, they bring about a state of affairs which is consistent with what Christ would achieve through his death upon the cross and his resurrection. The miracles bring about the restoration to wholeness of broken, sinful and weak men and women. And that same restoration remains an integral part of the Christian understanding of the cross. The ideas of healing and salvation are closely linked. We have been wounded by sin, and need to be healed.

But the English words 'healing' and 'salvation' seem totally unrelated. This brings us to an important point. Bible translators face all sorts of problems. One of the most difficult has to do with translating Greek words which have more than one meaning. A classic example might be Jesus' famous reply to Nicodemus, 'No-one can see the kingdom of God unless he is born again' (John 3:3). The Greek word here translated as 'again' (*anōthen*) has two root meanings – 'again' and 'from above' – obliging translators of this passage to insert footnotes noting both possibilities. But which is right, and which is wrong? Which is the intended meaning? It is actually quite possible that both meanings are intended. To be born again *is* to be born from above. Our first birth is from below, an earthly and natural event. Our second birth is from above, a heavenly and spiritual event.

The same problem arises with a Greek verb which is regularly used in the gospels to denote the idea of salvation. To illustrate the problem we may consider Luke 7:50. Jesus here tells the 'woman who had lived a sinful life' (verse 37): 'Your faith has saved you; go in peace.' The Greek verb *sōzein*, here translated as 'save', has a range of meanings, however, including those of 'heal' or 'make whole'. The passage in question could equally well be translated as 'Your faith has made you whole' or 'Your faith has healed you.'[39]

So how does the image of healing help us make sense of the cross? First, it affirms the transformative power of the suffering of Christ. It is by his wounds that we are healed (Isaiah 53:5). We shall be exploring this theme further in the next chapter. Second, it tells us that the healing process itself is a powerful visual aid for the gospel. It casts light on the way in which God is binding up our sin-inflicted wounds and healing our spiritual infirmities.

Perhaps the neatest definition of healing is *restoration to health*. In other words, sickness represents a lapse from a healthy state, caused by the invasion of some virus or the failure of some bodily organ. We realize that we are sick because we are able to compare ourselves with our normal healthy states, and notice that something is amiss. There is a standard, a norm, which allows us to discover that all is not well. The gospel tells us that we are sinful (ill), and that we require salvation (healing). The way we are isn't the way we are meant to be. We are sick – but we could be healthy, if we were to entrust ourselves to the gentle care of the wounded physician of Calvary. And, on account of the faithfulness of God to his promises, and the efficacy of what Christ achieved on the cross, we may hope that, although we are at present ill, we shall one day be whole again. This point was made especially well by Martin Luther, who wrote:

> It is just like someone who is sick, and who believes the doctor who promises his full recovery. In the meantime, he obeys the doctor's orders in the hope of the promised recovery. And he abstains from those things which he has been told to lay off, so that he may in no way hinder the promised return to health . . . Now is this sick man well? In fact, he is both sick and well at the same time. He is sick in reality – but he is well on account of the sure promise of the doctor, whom he trusts, and who reckons him as already being cured.[40]

This image also helps us think about the sort of people who are Christians. Augustine once likened the church to a hospital. It is a community of sick people, united by their willingness to acknowledge their sin and their hope and trust in the skill of the physicians to whose care they are committed. Critics of Christianity often say that faith is some kind of crutch. By this they mean that it is the sort of thing that inadequate people lean on. They dismiss Christians as inadequate and weak, unable to get through life without support.

But if your leg is broken, you need a crutch. You might as well be honest about it, and admit it. The gospel declares that *all* have sinned, that *all* have fallen short of the glory of God; that *all* – to continue our analogy – have broken legs; that *all* need crutches. Pretending that we aren't sinners is about as sensible as pretending that we haven't got blood poisoning, when all the symptoms are already there. This act of denial may save your face, but it won't save your life. Admitting to illness is the prerequisite for healing. No admission of illness: no prescription of life-saving drugs and therapy. No admission of sin: no divine forgiveness.

Christians are simply those who have the honesty and integrity to admit that they need help and care. And they rejoice in the fact that they have found it in Christ, through the grace of God. Even in the New Testament period, people were complaining about the sort of people who became Christians.[41] How outrageous that God should call the weak and the foolish of the world! But, as Jesus reminds us, 'it is not the healthy who need a doctor, but the sick' (Mark 2:17). It takes guts to admit that you are ill, and need the kind of treatment the gospel makes available.

But this image of the cross also allows us to trust the credentials of the physician, to whose care we have entrusted ourselves. One of the most moving passages in the Old Testament is a prophecy concerning the suffering of the servant of God (Isaiah 53:1–12). It is through the suffering of this servant that others will be brought to wholeness. And as the Christian church read this passage in the light of the sufferings of Jesus upon the cross, there was suddenly no mystery about the identity of this mysterious sufferer. Those who witnessed the crucifixion saw this prophecy fulfilled before their eyes.

> Surely he took up our infirmities
>   and carried our sorrows,
> yet we considered him stricken by God,
>   smitten by him, and afflicted.
> But he was pierced for our transgressions,
>   he was crushed for our iniquities;
> the punishment that brought us peace was
>   upon him,
>   and by his wounds we are healed.

The theme to emerge clearly from this passage is simple: Christ took upon himself our sorrows, fears and punishment. As we look upon Christ, dying upon the cross, we can see the deep-rooted problems of the fallen human race exposed and dealt with. And we, who share that fallen human nature with all its failings and weaknesses, can gain insight and inspiration by reflecting on that cross.

A phrase from Carl Jung comes to mind in this context. 'Only the wounded physician can heal.' Christ is the wounded physician of Calvary. He heals us by entering into our human situation, and sharing its woes and its wounds. And by doing this, he gives new hope and meaning to those who pass this way after him. It is an enormous consolation to know that God suffered in Christ. Knowing that God understands the joys and woes of being human makes it easy to entrust ourselves to the care of such a physician. We can relate to him with confidence. Why? Because he has travelled down our road before us. He has shared our infirmities and pain.

A friend of mine has asthma. He always makes a point of seeing the same doctor at his local medical centre. 'Everyone else treats me as if I was making a lot of fuss about nothing,' he said. 'But this guy understands me.' Why? Because he too is an asthma sufferer! You can be sure of a sympathetic reception, genuine compassion, and a real awareness of the possibilities for treatment. If you've had a problem yourself, it's very easy to relate to the needs of others going through the same thing. There's a real piece of theological insight nestling in that observation. That's why we feel we can trust the God who offers us healing through the cross.

And finally, we need to be aware that healing may take time. And while that process of healing is taking place, we are in a kind of intermediate state. We are both ill, in that we are still not healthy, and healthy, in that we are on the road to recovery. Just as you can think of someone on the mend as being ill and healthy at the same time, so you can think of forgiven believers as simultaneously sinful and righteous. Luther makes this point:

> So such a person is at one and the same time both a sinner and righteous. He is a sinner in reality, but righteous by the sure imputation and promise of God that he will continue to deliver him from sin until he has completely cured him. So he is entirely healthy in hope, but a sinner in reality.

The presence of sin or doubt, then, is not necessarily a symptom of a lapse from faith, or of an imperfect commitment to God.[42] It can be nothing more than a reflection of our continuing real struggle against sin. And this struggle is an essential component of the process of justification and renewal. Let Luther have the final word on this point. 'In ourselves, we are sinners, and yet through faith we are righteous by the imputation of God. For we trust him who promises to deliver us. And in the meantime, we struggle so that sin may not overwhelm us. We try to stand up to it until God finally takes it away from us.'

These, then, are five images of salvation – images which open up the meaning of the cross and resurrection, and allow us to discover how they transform our vision of the world and ourselves. Each casts light on a different aspect of life. Each has a distinctive and vital contribution to make to our understanding and proclamation of the gospel. These images are God's gift to his people, to help us make sense of what has happened to us through faith. They are also there to help us lay before the world the astonishing news of what God has already done in Christ. And they point ahead to what he could still do to that tired and weary world. The cross changes things. It changes them in a big way.

Who Is Changed by the Cross— God or We?

The cross and resurrection may be said to mark the dawn of a new era in the history of the world. Socrates may have shown us how to die with dignity; Jesus Christ shows us how to die in hope. The image of change is central to making sense of the cross. The previous chapter explored a number of ways of imaging or visualizing this change – such as healing. There is, however, a question which has been implicit in a lot of what has been said, but it ought to be addressed directly. Who is changed by the cross – God, or us?

We can begin to answer this question by making a distinction between *subjective* and *objective* approaches to the cross. A subjective understanding of the cross argues that the cross changes us. Our perception of things is altered. It is not the situation that changes; it is the way we see that situation. An objective understanding argues that it is God who, in some way, is affected by the cross. The situation outside of us is changed by the cross. The situation, not just our perception of it, is altered. To bring out this distinction more clearly, let us look at examples of each.

There is a purely subjective approach to the cross which is sometimes called the 'moral' or 'exemplarist' view. This became especially fashionable in rationalist circles in the nineteenth century. It goes like this. The cross changes the way we think about God. It educates us, by showing us what God is really like. Left to ourselves, we would have very muddled understandings of who God is, and what he is like. The cross is educational, in that it liberates us from false understandings of God. For example, we might believe that God does not love us. But the cross declares otherwise, and so our perception of the situation changes.

An example of a purely objective approach to the cross is provided by what is sometimes called the *Christus Victor* theory of the atonement. (The two Latin words mean 'Christ the Victor'.) This is a way of thinking about the cross, especially popular in the early Middle Ages, which highlights the victory won by God over Satan by the resurrection of Christ. It is a powerful image, which many find helpful. But it has its weaknesses. The main flaw concerns the role of human beings in redemption. We tend to be treated as nothing more than the prize over which God and Satan were fighting. We are seen as booty, not as persons. As a result of God's victory, the situation changes. We are no longer under the authority of Satan, but under the dominion of God. The situation changes – but we aren't much affected by it. We are still being treated as possessions.

It will be obvious that both these approaches are

inadequate. Responsible approaches to the cross remain faithful to the New Testament insistence that the cross changes both the way things are, and the way we see things. There are both objective and subjective aspects to the cross. Our relationship to God is changed by the cross, as is our experience of God. Inside and outside, the cross makes a difference. Let's explore this point with reference to two analogies.

The first is drawn from the writings of Karl Marx, specifically the *Economic and Philosophical Manuscripts* of 1844. At first sight, this might seem an unlikely resource. However, it has considerable value in contemporary attempts to defend and justify the Christian faith. Marx argues that the human situation is characterized by *alienation*.[43] He distinguishes two different kinds of alienation.[44] The first is alienation from your rights and your property – a sort of *objective* alienation. You are alienated. The second is *subjective*, a more psychological or existential kind of alienation. You feel alienated from yourself. Marx's insight is quite simple: you *feel* alienated because you *are* alienated. If your social and economic situation is disastrous, you are going to feel bad about it.

Marx then goes on to argue the case for a social and economic revolution. Part of his argument is of interest to us. No amount of tinkering around with our feelings, he declares, is going to solve our problems. They are but symptoms of a deeper problem, which remains unresolved by emotional therapy. If you are oppressed and exploited, you are going to feel alienated. The only way you are going to get rid of this feeling of alienation is by changing your social and economic situation. An objective change will result in a subjective change.

A less theoretical analogy may give more substance

to the point. Suppose you are in serious debt. Perhaps you have a credit card, and have allowed yourself to run up massive charges. Or you have taken out a loan, and the bank has decided to foreclose. Or you felt the need to give someone in your family a really good holiday, which involved borrowing a large sum of money from a loan shark. And now you are in serious trouble. Your creditor is demanding immediate payment. The debt must be settled at once. Legal action is threatened by the credit card company and the bank; the loan shark is crudely hinting at physical violence, unless you pay up. And the simple truth is that you cannot pay. There is nothing that you can do to earn enough money to settle the debt. And, deep down, you *know* you can never pay.[45]

Perhaps you have been through such a crisis. Perhaps you have stood alongside a friend as he or she wrestled with this kind of distressing predicament. If you have been fortunate enough never to have experienced such a dilemma, try to imagine how you would feel in that situation. You might feel depressed and anxious. You might feel overwhelmed by a pervasive sense of despair, mingled with hopelessness and helplessness. You might feel numbed by a sense of powerlessness.

Now imagine how you would react if some friends listened to you describing these feelings. Then, like modern Job's comforters, they harangued you like this: 'Pull yourself together! There's nothing wrong with you at all! It's all in your mind. You're obsessed by delusions. Think positive, and get on with life.' You would be shocked. Your situation is being treated as something imaginary, not something real. You are being told in no uncertain terms that there is no objective cause for your emotional state. If your friends really wanted to help, they could bale you out of your debts. They could alter your objective situation by paying off the huge sums of money you owed. Then you would *feel* better!

Now these analogies make a very important theological point. We *feel* alienated from God because we *are* alienated from God. We *feel* ourselves to be guilty in his sight because we *are* guilty in his sight. A purely subjective approach to the meaning of the cross is deficient. It lacks something vital. It fails to deal with the vital fact that the cross changes things. To use the imagery of healing we noted earlier: if you are seriously ill, you are likely to be depressed by it. Someone who offers you emotional therapy ('You'll feel better soon. Don't worry about it. Relax.'), but who fails to address the disease which is slowly but surely killing you, can hardly be said to have redeemed your situation. The subjective reassurance bears no relation to the objective state of things. You are being deceived.

A responsible approach to the cross brings together these aspects of the matter. We feel guilty because we are guilty – but we can rejoice at feeling forgiven through the cross, because we have been forgiven through the cross. There has been a real change outside us, which brings about a real change in our experience of God. Our feelings match up with the real situation – and both the situation and our feelings are transformed by what God has done for us through Christ.[46] That also applies to feelings of doubt, which trouble many Christians.

The cross and doubt

What is Christian doubt? It isn't scepticism – the decision to doubt everything as a matter of principle. Nor is it unbelief – the deliberate decision to reject Christianity. Doubt, like sin, is a common experience for most Christians.[47] Why?

The basic difficulty here is the human desire to know things for certain. We want to be absolutely sure about everything – the Christian faith included. But no-one can ever have this kind of certainty about God. The atheist and the Christian believe very different things about whether there is a God. But they both take their positions as a matter of faith. Neither can prove their position for certain. Recognizing this point puts doubt in its proper perspective. No belief about God can be known with the kind of knock-down certainty that we would like. So doubt is natural. It's understandable that we should wonder if we have got things right. Doubt becomes a problem only if you let it worry you.

Doubt is not an intellectual difficulty with God. It is something more fundamental than that. It is the basic human instinct *not* to trust God. This instinct naturally allies itself with any intellectual problems to hand. But it is this self-centred instinct to turn away from God which is the real issue. Doubt is not so much a problem of the human mind. It is the expression of a force or power which engulfs the entire sinful human person, and draws him or her away from God.

Two images of what Christ achieved on the cross are helpful here. First, let us return to images drawn from a battlefield. Think of doubt, like sin, as an enemy. In fact, sin and doubt are rather like two sides of the same coin, both hostile forces, which try to disrupt the Christian life. Think about a military commander trying to neutralize the threat of a hostile army. He might try to prevent that army from reaching vital supplies of ammunition, fuel and food. If it is starved of these resources, it would soon grind to a halt, and cease being a serious threat. So doubt tries to drive a wedge between the believing Christian and the promises of God. An army marches on its stomach. Christian faith marches on the promises of God. Think of doubt trying to starve you of the food of faith, by causing you to distrust the goodness of God or his faithfulness to his promises. If it succeeds, you have been cut off from the spiritual resources you need to keep going in the Christian life.

Christ gained a triple victory over sin, death and doubt on the cross. Try to imagine the scene as Christ died. People were expecting God to intervene and do something dramatic. Maybe they thought he would send in an army of angels to remove Christ from that cross. But nothing of the sort happened. Jesus felt abandoned by God. And he died, without any sign of God intervening. Death, sin and doubt seemed to have gained the upper hand.

But the resurrection changed everything. Death was swallowed up in victory. Sin was defeated. And doubt was put in its proper place. The crucifixion led people to believe that God was not there; but the resurrection demonstrated his presence, purpose and power at Calvary. The promise of God triumphed over doubt, yet the struggle goes on. Christian believers still have to contend with the power of sin, the sure and frightening knowledge of our death, and the assaults of doubts. As we saw in the last chapter, the victory gained by Christ is for real, but it has yet to break in fully to our human world. The backbone of spiritual resistance to the gospel may have been broken. But opposition still remains – the 'old Adam', lingering within us. Doubt is a symptom of that continuing resistance to God, and a reminder of our need to trust more fully in the promises of God.

The second helpful set of images is drawn from the hospital. I remember once reading Betty McDonald's *The Plague and I*, which superbly evokes the atmosphere of a sanatorium for long-term patients. Having discovered that she is ill, McDonald is admitted to the sanatorium. Eventually, she makes a full recovery. But it takes a long time. It isn't as if she is ill one day, and the next day she has recovered. Recovery is a slow process. The patient gradually moves from a position which could be described as 'ill' to one which could be described as 'well'. The symptoms of illness do not suddenly vanish. They persist. But their pattern changes. They become less frequent and less intense. But they never entirely disappear. Someone who has had malaria knows only too well how its symptoms can reappear, even though they have been 'cured'.

Doubt is a symptom of our old and unredeemed human nature. It is characteristic of the sinful human tendency to trust in ourselves. What Christ achieved through the cross and resurrection enables our wounded nature to be healed. But even as we are being healed by grace, the symptoms of our illness persist. We remain sinners. The power of sin is waning, and its presence is being reduced. But it is still there – as is doubt. Doubt remains as long as sin remains. But it need not be a problem. It is like an attention-seeking child. Pay it attention, and it demands more.

Those who are plagued by doubt could be said to have an attitude problem. They refuse to acknowledge the fact that everyone – whether Christian or atheist –

lives in a world in which nothing vital can be proved for certain. They become obsessed with the idea that things have to be proved beyond doubt before they can be taken seriously. But life is not like that. The key to coping with doubt is to adopt a relaxed and realistic attitude towards it. See it as something more or less inevitable, a reminder of the continuing presence of sin and our continuing need for grace. A long healing process lies ahead. Our illness is long-term and serious. But it is not fatal. What Christ achieved on the cross can make us whole. We must learn to entrust ourselves to his tender care, in the knowledge that he who began a good work within us will one day bring it to its glorious completion.[48]

The cross, then, does more than tell us about our situation; it offers to change it. A physician who diagnoses a serious illness brings only bad news – unless there is the will, the ability and the resources to cure that illness. The good news of the gospel is that its diagnosis of our situation is followed immediately by a declaration of God's will and ability to change things. So how do we connect up with the cross, and allow it to transform our situation? How can it break into our lives?

The Cross in Everyday Life

How can something which happened long, long ago and far, far away have any relevance to us today? How can believing that some theory is true change your life? How can intellectual assent to something cause us to rise, renewed and forgiven in the sight of God? In short: how can we link up with the cross, and all that it means?

To answer this question, we need to rediscover the meaning of that short yet difficult word 'faith'. In the course of their Christian lives, many people get no further than treating faith as some kind of belief. It is intellectual assent. It is accepting that certain things are true. To believe in God is to believe that God exists. To have faith in the cross is to believe that the cross really happened, and is not the figment of someone's overactive imagination. And that, according to this common-sense notion of faith, is all that there is to it.

In fact, the Christian concept of faith possesses a

depth totally overlooked by this shallow understanding. In everyday English, heavily influenced by the ideas of the Enlightenment, the word 'faith' means something like 'a lower form of knowledge'. But in the Christian sense of the word, it possesses a much deeper meaning. There are three main elements to the Christian understanding of faith:

1. Faith is about believing that certain things are true. Thus when we say that we believe in God, we are at the very least believing in his existence. Or if we were to say that we believed in the promises of God, we could mean simply that we recognize or accept that the promises really are there. In this sense, faith is basically assent. 'I believe in God' means something like 'I believe that there is a God', or 'I think that God exists.' This is an essential starting point. Before we can begin to say anything about what God is like, we need to assume that there is a God in the first place. Yet many people outside the Christian faith have the impression that there is nothing more to Christian faith than assent to God's existence. Christian belief is little more than running through a checklist of propositions – such as those contained in the creeds. In itself, this is an inadequate understanding of faith.

2. Faith is trust. When I say that I believe in the promises of God, I am declaring that I trust them. It is more than a recognition that these promises exist; it is an awareness that they can be trusted and relied upon. Faith is not something purely intellectual, enlightening the mind while leaving the heart untouched. Faith is the response of our whole persons to the person of God. It is a joyful reaction on our part to the overwhelming divine love we see revealed in Jesus Christ.

It is the simple response of leaving all to follow Jesus. Faith is both our recognition that something wonderful has happened through the life, death and resurrection of Jesus Christ, and our response to what has happened. Faith realizes that God loves us, and responds to that love. Faith trusts in the promising God. But there is still more to faith than this.

3. Faith is entry into the promises of God. Having recognized that the promises exist, and that they can be trusted, it is necessary to act upon them – to receive what they promise, and benefit from them. I may believe that God is promising me forgiveness of sins; I may trust that promise; but unless I respond to that promise, I shall not obtain forgiveness. The first two stages of faith prepare the way for the third; without it they are incomplete.

An analogy may make this point clearer. Consider a bottle of penicillin, the famous antibiotic identified by Alexander Fleming, and first produced for clinical use at Oxford. The drug was responsible for saving the lives of countless individuals who would otherwise have died from various forms of blood poisoning. Think of the three stages to faith like this. I may *accept* that the bottle exists. I may *trust* in its ability to cure blood poisoning. But nothing will change unless I *receive* the drug which it contains. I must allow it to destroy the bacteria which are slowly but surely killing me. Otherwise, I have not benefited from my faith in it.

It is this third element of faith which is of vital importance in making sense of the cross. Just as faith links a bottle of penicillin to the cure of blood poisoning, so faith forges a link between the cross and resurrection of Jesus Christ and ourselves. Faith unites us with the risen Christ, and makes available to us everything that he gained through his obedience and resurrection – such as forgiveness, grace and eternal life. These 'benefits of Christ' – to use a classical way of speaking – become ours through faith. They are not detached from the person of Christ, as if we could have them in isolation; rather, they are given together with his real and redeeming presence within us, brought about by faith.

Faith, then, is not just assent to an abstract set of doctrines. Rather, it is a 'wedding ring' (Luther), pointing to mutual commitment and union between Christ and the believer. It is the response of the whole person of the believer to God. This leads in turn to the real and personal presence of Christ in the believer. 'To know Christ is to know his benefits,' wrote Philip Melanchthon, Luther's colleague at Wittenberg. John Calvin makes this point with characteristic clarity. 'Having ingrafted us into his body, Christ makes us partakers, not only of all his benefits, but also of himself.' Christ, Calvin insists, is not 'received merely in the understanding and imagination. For the promises offer him, not so that we end up with the mere sight and knowledge of him, but that we enjoy a true communication of him.'[49]

So how are we to make sense of this central theme of Christian thought – that faith unites the believer both to the person and the benefits of Christ? The most helpful analogy for understanding this vital point is that of a human marriage, with faith being seen as analogous to the marriage bond uniting husband and wife. Martin Luther states this principle clearly in *The Liberty of a Christian*, written in 1520:

Faith unites the soul with Christ as a bride is united with her bridegroom. As Paul teaches us, Christ and the soul become one flesh by this mystery (Ephesians 5:31–32). And if they are one flesh, and if the marriage is for real . . . then it follows that everything that they have is held in common, whether good or evil. So the believer can boast of and glory in whatever Christ possesses, as though it were his or her own. And whatever the believer has, Christ claims as his own. Let us see how this works out, and see how it benefits us. Christ is full of grace, life and salvation. The human soul is full of sin, death and damnation. Now let faith come between them. Sin, death and damnation will be Christ's. And grace, life and salvation will be the believer's.

A human marriage is no legal fiction. It is a real and vital relationship between two persons, involving personal union, mutual commitment, a common life and a sharing of goods. Precisely this relationship is established between the believer and the risen Christ through faith. The believer comes to be in Christ.[50] A dynamic bond is forged between the believing human being and the redeeming Christ, bringing in its wake a partaking of all that he won for us by his obedience.

So how do we benefit from what Christ achieved on the cross? It is at this point that our reflections about the nature of faith are of central importance. Faith is the bond which unites us to Christ, and allows him to become personally present within us. At the same time, it unites us with all the resources and privileges which he purchased for us on the cross. Faith is like a channel, through which the righteousness of Christ becomes ours, so that we become righteous in the sight of God. It is like a hand, which reaches out to take hold of the treasures which Christ offers us – such as forgiveness, joy and hope. It is like an open mouth, which feeds on all that Christ bestows upon us as nourishment – such as liberation, salvation and eternal life.

If faith is the hand which takes hold of Christ, then it must be stressed that Christ is offered to us as a gift. The gospel constantly stresses that everything which we could never achieve or ever hope to purchase is offered to us freely. That is what grace is all about – the graciousness of God in giving us things we do not deserve and dared not hope for.

We are now in a position to see how this links up with the five sets of images of redemption that we discussed in chapter 4. Let's follow three of them through. The other two are left for you to work out.

1. A battlefield. God has achieved a military victory through the death and resurrection of Jesus. The fruits of this victory are offered to us, as a gift. We are being invited to share in its spoils, even though we did not ourselves take part in the battle. Those spoils include freedom from oppression. The issue of that struggle has already been decided. We are being invited to enter into a new world and a new era, neither created nor won through our efforts, but offered to us as a gift.

2. A relationship. Most of us know from personal experience how easily relationships can go wrong – through misunderstanding, sheer stupidity, or through a lack of proper consideration for the feelings of others. But a broken or disrupted relationship is potentially a *renewed* relationship. That process of renewal is often painful, involving the distressing process of bringing the hurt, along with what caused it, out into the open. But the bitterness of alienation is transformed through reconciliation, as the offended offers forgiveness to the offender. But that forgiveness must be accepted, if the relationship is to be transformed. Forgiveness is a two-way street. Think of faith as saying, 'Yes – and I'm sorry' to the offer of forgiveness from the loved one whom you have put through the bitterness of a ruptured relationship.

3. A hospital. When Jesus approaches the man who has been crippled from birth at the pool of Bethzatha, he asks him a simple question. 'Do you *want* to get well?'[51] Faith is about saying yes to the offer of healing from Christ the wounded physician. It is about accepting the offer of a life-giving drug, without which we will die. Acceptance and trust prepare the way for the final component of faith – entering into the promise, and receiving what it offers. God offers to cure us, to make us whole, on account of what Christ achieved on the cross. But we must accept that offer of healing, if things are to change.

The same insights can be applied to the images drawn from the lawcourts or prisons. You are being offered a pardon for your sins. It's up to you to accept it. Your prison door has been flung open, and you are free to leave – but you must walk out of that cell, and accept your freedom.

But a difficulty might seem to arise here. If everything is offered to us as a gift, it might seem that we could accept these gifts, and remain unchanged as people. God would give his gifts to us sinners – but sinners we could remain. This brings us to discuss the transformational character of faith.

Faith, as we have seen, unites us to Christ. It

establishes a bond of union, at the deepest and most personal level, between Christ and the believer. And that personal relationship holds the key to our development as Christians. For by being united to Christ, we become like Christ. Through the power of the Holy Spirit, the presence of Christ within us comes to change us, so that we grow to be like Christ himself.

Faith changes us, and makes us more like Christ himself. To come to faith is not simply to believe some new ideas; nor is it simply to put your trust in God. It is to do both these things, and, by being united to the risen Christ, to be transformed and renewed by his presence, and refashioned after his image and likeness. We do not, however, lose our individuality as a result. Rather, our individuality is brought to fulfilment through relating to Christ. The great medieval theologian Thomas Aquinas once wrote: 'Grace does not abolish nature, but perfects it.' An immature or un-activated faith may just believe that certain things about God are true – and nothing more; but a living faith is united to, and transformed by, its object – the living and loving God.

Relating the cross to individual needs

In chapter four, we saw how five groups of images help us to make sense of the cross. Of course, these images are not mutually inconsistent. The cross spells freedom *and* healing *and* forgiveness, for example. These three images are complementary. They build up to give a complete whole. To be transformed by the cross and resurrection of Jesus Christ is to be liberated, to be healed and to be forgiven – and more.

I met the man I shall call Pete late on a November

evening in southern California. I had just given an address to a large group of students at the local state university in San Diego, when he introduced himself to me. It had been a long day, and I was tired. I did not listen to him with quite the attention he deserved. But what he said made me wake up. He described to me in great detail the mess in which he had found himself. I can never hope to match his eloquence, nor capture the poignancy of his tale, but the gist of what he said was this.

He had been a cocaine addict. He was trapped in his situation with no means of escape, and he knew it. It seemed that nothing he could do was able to change the way things were. It was as if invisible forces were moulding his life, bending his will to fit their needs. His body was sapped of hope, and drained dry of any will to live. He had already committed numerous acts of petty theft in order to finance his habit. At times, he had been tempted to kill, if it would have ensured a regular supply of the white powder that had become the focus of his existence. All his hopes and fears centred on his craving. It was destroying him, slowly but surely. In his mind, he knew that this was the case. But he just couldn't kick the habit. He was hooked. And recognizing that he was hooked didn't seem to help. Just knowing about his problem didn't solve it. His will was broken. He used to look back with dreadful and tearful nostalgia to his days of lost innocence – before he discovered the white powder. They seemed so far away. And it seemed that they would never return. He had gone too far down the road of narcotic addiction to return. An utterly bleak and desolate future seemed to lie ahead. Every day that dawned seemed dark with despondency and devoid of hope.

I remember this conversation for two reasons. First,

on account of the eloquence with which this young man managed to portray the indescribable bleakness of a cocaine addict's life. Although I have never had this problem, he described it so well that I felt that I had entered into his world, and was sharing its grim and hopeless void. The sense of being utterly oppressed and dominated by something over which we have no control came home to me with a power and a force I had never experienced before. For a few brief minutes, I shared the mental world of the no-hopers and outcasts. It was a frightening experience.

But the second reason I recall this conversation concerns its final outcome. After having described his situation so vividly, Pete remarked 'Sounds kinda grim, doesn't it?' I could only agree. 'Well,' he continued, 'I'm free now. I've broken the habit. You wanna know how?' And he told me of how he had become converted to Christianity. He had found liberation in his conversion. Somehow, the forces which had compelled him to his addiction seemed to have been neutralized. He was healed. He became a whole person. The clouds lifted from his life. 'I guess I got hooked on Jesus instead – and I just want you to know it is truly awesome!' were his parting words, as he wandered happily off to rejoin his friends.

Not everyone is a cocaine addict. But many of us can recognize something of Pete's story in our own lives. All of us are trapped in situations of one sort or another. Pete was addicted to a white powder. Others are addicted to lesser, but real, habits. Habits like the need for praise, the quest for status, and the search for recognition. Pete is an extreme case of a universal problem.

But the real relevance of this little story lies in the way in which Pete's story brings together two images of restoration – liberation and healing. He had been liberated from his addiction, and healed as a person. The two images overlap. They interpenetrate and interrelate. The other images discussed in this chapter follow the same pattern. They are all there in the crucifixion and resurrection of Jesus Christ. They haven't been imposed upon the cross; they have been discerned within it.

In the eighteenth century, Isaac Newton made an important discovery in his rooms at Trinity College, Cambridge. He noticed that a beam of white light could be split into its constituent colours by a glass prism. The same effect which gave rise to the colours of the rainbow could be reproduced by a piece of glass in the laboratory. But what did the glass prism actually do? It merely split white light up into its constituent elements – red, orange, yellow, green, blue, indigo and violet. Those colours were always there in a beam of white light; the prism merely allowed them to be isolated, and examined individually. The apparently white light of the sun was shown to be made up of many different colours of light in combination. The prism allowed them to be separated out from each other. In nature, all were combined; in the laboratory, they could be split up.

The same is true of theology, which breaks the message of the cross and resurrection down into its constituent parts, so that they can be examined individually. The message of the cross is a unity – but it is a complex unity. It is by examining its individual components one by one that the whole message can be better appreciated and understood. But these components are not invented; they are uncovered. They are not the product of some overactive theological imagination. They are already present, awaiting our analysis, in the 'message of the cross'. All that the theologian has done is to isolate them, so that each can be studied individually.

But the story of white light and prisms did not stop there. It was soon discovered that the same prism which split white light up into its component colours could recombine those colours, and reproduce the original beam of white light. An experiment was devised which proved this neatly. A beam of white light was passed through one prism, which split it up into a glorious multicoloured spectrum. This rainbow of colours was then passed through a second prism, identical to the first – which promptly recombined them, to give a second beam of white light.

The same is true of theology. Having analysed the message of the cross, and identified the images of grace within it in order that they can be better understood, the theologian recombines them, to give the message of the cross. It is the same message as before – but it is a message which is now far better grasped and appreciated. So why bother with this analysis? What is the point of it?

The answer is as simple as it is important: because we need to relate the message to its audience. We need to ensure that the message of the cross is as effectively proclaimed as possible. And that means asking what points of contact there are for the gospel. How can we make sure that it scratches where people itch? To lapse into jargon: the gospel proclamation must be receptor-orientated. That is, it must be addressed to the opportunities which await it among its audience.

While all the components of the message of the cross are relevant to the human situation, individual human beings will have different specific needs. For example, someone may have a genuine fear of dying. The gospel needs to be tailored to that situation. Does that mean reducing the gospel? No. It is to recognize that this is where the rubber hits the road in this particular life. The rest will follow, as the implications of the healing brought by the gospel begin to dawn in the new life of faith. The component of the message of the cross which addresses this fear of death is like the thin end of a wedge – it secures a point of entry. It is an emphasis within the message, not a reduction of the message to a single point. It is but a starting point – a highly relevant starting point, to be sure. It is a Trojan horse which enters the camp of unbelief before throwing open its gates to the full resources of the gospel. The rest can, and will, follow.

So breaking down the 'message of the cross' into its components allows us to gain an idea of the nature of the resources at our disposal as we seek to proclaim the gospel more effectively. There is a real and urgent need to particularize the gospel proclamation in individual human lives. We cannot adopt a hopelessly generalized approach to the gospel – for example, by talking about 'liberation' in vague and indefinite terms. We need to ask: from what does this person, to whom I am trying to explain the gospel, need to be liberated? That means getting to know people and their needs. It means using images and language adapted to their situation. Paul brilliantly uses images drawn from the urban life of his readers. Jesus deploys analogies drawn superbly from the everyday life of rural Galilean communities.[52] They knew what they wanted to say, and they knew how to say it. We ought to do the same.

The issue, then, is that of contextualization. There must be a serious and sustained attempt to make sure that the full impact of the cross and resurrection is brought to bear upon an individual. In the first place, this means knowing the full resources that the gospel can bring to bear on that situation. In the second, it means knowing the circumstances of the individual, to make sure that the message of the cross fully enmeshes and engages with their needs. So know your gospel – and know your friends.

Points of contact for the cross

Any book on Christian theology runs the risk of sinking into the sands of theory. Reflection on the cross and resurrection of Christ often degenerates into inwardness and abstraction, instead of rising into concrete action in the world. The cross means so much that it cannot be reduced to abstract theories, to a kind of 'knowledge which rattles around inside our heads' (Calvin). It must shape our thinking and our living, alerting us to new ways of seeing and serving those whom we meet in the world.

In bringing this chapter to a close, we are going to reflect on some of the fears and anxieties to which fallen human nature is prone. These are for real. And the cross casts light on them. They are like vignettes, little snapshots of the sadder and more distressing side of human life, which are lent new dignity and distinction through knowing that Christ passed this way before. They are the points of contact with a sad and suffering world, by which the joy of faith may begin to be understood. Let us take an example, and work it through. The example I have selected seems to be deeply embedded in modern western culture – the fear of death. How do the cross and resurrection of Christ connect up with someone frightened of dying?

Woody Allen is perhaps one of the most important modern American film-makers to deal with this morbid human fear. In *Hannah and her Sisters*, he presents us with an unforgettable moment. A man wakes up, in the middle of a lonely night, to confront the unwelcome fact that he is going to die – perhaps quite soon. 'My God!', he screams, 'I'm going to DIE!' There comes a moment in the life of just about every human being when terrifying thoughts of death flash through their minds, often late at night. And they cannot cope with them.

Very often, the death of a close friend or relative proves to be a turning point in people's lives. The death of a friend can lead to the birth of faith, as they realize that death is an issue which cannot be avoided for ever. It has to be faced. And many discover that they just cannot cope with the awful reality of death. They devise all sorts of coping mechanisms to allow them to live, without having to confront the fact that one day, they will die. Ernst Becker's famous book *The Denial of Death* makes this point very clearly and powerfully. Many are secret prisoners of the fear of death.

The cross liberates us from this fear. It acts as a powerful antidote to our natural tendency to be frightened or anxious about our situation in the world. It allows us to face death with a quiet and calm confidence, knowing that its sting has been drawn by the cross, and victory given through the resurrection. The letter to the Hebrews makes this point powerfully. It declares that Jesus died in order that he might 'free all those who all their lives were held in slavery by their fear of death' (Hebrews 2:14–15).

Now notice what this approach is saying. It isn't saying, 'Let's pretend that death has been defeated.

111

Let's pretend that its power has been broken. And let's live our lives as if death should not worry us.' That would amount to closing our eyes to the harsh realities of life, and living in a make-believe world of fantasy. It would be like stepping into a fairy tale, or into an arcade game of dungeons and dragons. No! It is saying something very different indeed. It is saying, 'Through the cross and resurrection of Jesus Christ, the power of death has been broken. We have been given victory over death through Christ. We need not fear death any more, because on the cross, Christ grappled with it, and defeated it.' This is no pretend world of an over-excited and fertile human imagination. It is the real world of the gospel, given and guaranteed by God himself. And that knowledge ought to change us. It ought to transform the way we think and the way we live.

Death has been tamed. John Bunyan makes this point forcefully in *Pilgrim's Progress*, using a vivid storyline. Christian is walking down a road, when to his horror he notices a ferocious lion barring his path. There is no way that he can avoid the animal. Terrified, he draws closer. Then, to his delight, he notices that the lion is chained to a post. Someone has been that way before him, and tamed this fearsome beast. Although he must walk that same way, an earlier traveller has made the road safe for him. Someone else met that hostile creature before him, and disarmed it. Although the lion remains, the threat it once posed has been removed.

The cross liberates us from this malignant tyranny of death. It breaks its oppressive stranglehold over us. The New Testament resonates with the joyful realization that Christ lives – and that, because he lives, we shall live also. Christ's victory over the power and reality of death is our victory. Faith unites us to Christ, and all that he has achieved – including the defeat of death through death. It is true that in the midst of life, we are in death. But it is even more true that in the midst of death, we are in life. We begin to experience the eternal life made available to us through the gospel. And nothing – not even death itself – can take this away from us. 'Death has been swallowed up in victory' (1 Corinthians 15:54).

The message of the cross thus includes a component of vital importance to such a person. Their suffocating fear of dying can be defeated. The cross and resurrection of Christ can break its oppressive force over us – and open the way to claiming the good news of the death and resurrection of Jesus Christ in all its fulness.

Another approach might draw upon the widespread sense of alienation in modern society. Many people are profoundly aware that there is something wrong with the world. This awareness has very deep roots in modern western culture. There is a considerable body of literature devoted to the theme, which became especially important in the years following the Second World War.[53] Jean-Paul Sartre's *The Roads to Freedom*, Graham Greene's *Brighton Rock*, and Albert Camus' *The Outsider* all bear witness to this sense of estrangement. For Sartre and Camus, this alienation is an ineluctable feature of human nature. It can't be beaten. We are condemned to be alienated throughout the whole of our existence. Marx argued that it could be overcome by revolution. But the experience of societies which have undergone revolutions inspired and guided by Marxism is that alienation, far from being overcome, simply got worse.

The cross recognizes and addresses this sense of alienation. It argues that alienation is a symptom of human sin. It is not something which can be overcome by human effort. It requires something far more radical – the neutralization of human sin. The cross and resurrection demonstrate both the reality and power of that sin, but also the greater reality and power of the God who raised Christ Jesus from the dead.

These are just two of the many ways in which the cross and resurrection of Christ address common human experience – and, through faith, transfigure it into the redeeming knowledge of God. But the basic strategy is clear: to know your evangelistic opportunities, you need to know your theology on the one hand, and your audience on the other. And be assured that the cross and resurrection of Jesus Christ have the power and potential to relate to the people you know.

Conclusion

Corporations spend huge sums of money on designing logos. Advertising agencies are hired to conceive a logo which will express the qualities that the corporation wants to be associated with it in the public mind. These are usually qualities such as stability, reliability, progressiveness, or aggressiveness. This design will appear on their letterheads, on their products, and be prominently displayed at their national and local headquarters. In the 1980s the British Labour party, anxious to shake off its associations with an increasingly unpopular socialism, abandoned its traditional logo – a red banner – in favour of a red rose. A red banner conjured up now unacceptable images of such things as military parades in Red Square, Moscow. A rose evoked more tender and sensitive associations for the British people (traditionally noted for their love of gardening in general, and roses in particular). Militant associations were being rejected in favour of more compassionate and gentle ones, designed to project the image of a caring party. A logo tells us a lot about a corporation or organization – or, at least, about how they would like us to see them.

An organization which chose as its logo a hangman's noose, a firing squad, a gas chamber or an electric chair would accordingly seem to have taken leave of its senses. It would be sheer madness to choose an instrument of execution as a symbol of an organization. Its members would instantly be regarded as perverted, sick, having a morbid obsession with death, or having a nauseating interest in human suffering. It would be an advertising agency's nightmare. Only an organization determined to fail as quickly and spectacularly as possible would be mad enough to choose such a symbol.

And yet exactly such a symbol is universally recognized as the logo of Christianity. Christians are baptized with the sign of the cross. Churches and other Christian places of meeting do not merely include a cross; they are often built in the shape of a cross. Many Christians make the sign of the cross in times of danger or anxiety. The graves of Christians are marked with crosses. Careful studies of the origins and development of Christian symbolism have made it clear that the cross was seen as the symbol of the Christian gospel from the earliest of times.

But why? Why choose such a shocking and offensive symbol? Why not choose something more caring and compassionate? Throughout history, people have been scandalized by the cross. Many of its critics have argued that Christianity would have a much more favourable public image if it abandoned this absurdity. Even at the time of the New Testament, the bad press received by the cross was fully appreciated. Paul had no doubts that the Christian emphasis upon the cross was regarded as outrageous by two very significant groups of people. The Jews regarded it as scandalous, and the Greeks saw it as sheer madness (1 Corinthians 1:23).

So, given this widespread hostility in the world towards the cross, why not abandon it? Why not allow public relations and advertising agencies to come up with some new symbol of the gospel, which would be far more attractive to the general public? There has never been a shortage of people urging that this should be done. It would, we are told, be much easier to sell the gospel in the marketplace of life if it was more attractively packaged. Get rid of these unpleasant associations with death, suffering and execution. These are barbarous ideas, which needlessly offend the sensibilities of intelligent and cultured people. Then the Christian faith could achieve new heights of influence and acceptability.

But the cross has a relevance of its own, which must not be lost. It is a potent symbol of Christian realism. It declares that any outlook on life which cannot cope with the grim realities of suffering and death does not deserve to get a hearing. This symbol of suffering and death affirms that Christianity faces up to the grim, ultimate realities of life. It reminds us of something we must never be allowed to forget. God entered into our suffering and dying world in order to bring it newness of life. Those outside Christianity need to learn – need to be *told about* – its relevance and power for the tragic situation of humanity. It is a sign of a glory which is concealed. It confronts the worst which the world can offer, and points to – and makes possible – a better way. It stands as a symbol of hope which transfigures, in a world which is too often tinged with sadness and tears.

So consider the cross. A symbol of death? No. A symbol of suffering? No. A symbol of a world of death and suffering? Not quite. A symbol of hope in the midst of a world of death and suffering? Yes! A symbol of a God who is with us in this dark world, and beyond? Yes! In short, the cross stands for a hope that is for real, in a world that is for real. But that world will pass away, while that hope will remain for eternity.

Notes

1. Deuteronomy 17:6; 19:15; John 8:17.
2. The practice is referred to at Matthew 23:29.
3. Mark 5:22–24; 35–43.
4. John 11:1–44.
5. *E.g.*, 1 Corinthians 15:5–8.
6. A theory put forward, to general disbelief, by Baldensperger in a series of articles in *Revue d'Histoire et de Philosophie Religieuses* during the period 1932–34.
7. Genesis 22:4.
8. Joshua 3:2–3.
9. Hosea 6:2.
10. See Deuteronomy 21:23; Galatians 3:10–14.
11. Note the argument of Peter, in Acts 2:22–39, especially at verses 24, 31–33, 36.
12. The Greek word *apokalypsis* literally means 'removing a veil'. The idea is that God's face is finally revealed to his people, who up until now have had to make do with glimpses of God, seen from the back.

Cf. Exodus 33:23; John 1:18.

13. Mark 1:2–3. Note the quotation from Malachi 3:1, which makes it clear that the reference is to the coming of God to his people.

14. Matthew 3:13–14.

15. Mark 2:1–12.

16. For an excellent discussion of this vital point, see Wolfhart Pannenberg, *Jesus – God and Man* (London: SCM Press, 1968), pp. 53–66.

17. Mark 1:22.

18. John 15:13. It is worth reading 1 John 4:8–9 carefully. After declaring that God is love, John makes the point that this love is shown in action. God *showed* his love by sending Jesus to die for us.

19. The idea that God cannot suffer owes nothing to Scripture, but is due rather to the influence of Greek philosophy upon a number of influential Christian writers in the first few centuries after the resurrection. Modern theology has patiently recovered the idea of a God who suffers along with his people. For further details, see Richard Bauckham, 'Only the suffering God can help: divine passibility in modern theology', *Themelios* 9 (1984), pp. 6–12.

20. 1 Corinthians 15:3.

21. The interested reader is referred to C. F. D. Moule, *The Origins of Christology* (Cambridge: Cambridge University Press, 1977), for further discussion.

22. Mark 2:1–12.

23. See Alister E. McGrath, 'Resurrection and Incarnation: The Foundations of the Christian Faith', in *Different Gospels*, ed. A. Walker (London: Hodder and Stoughton, 1988), pp. 79-96.

24. There is a problem here relating to the English language, which has two words – righteousness and justice – where most others have just one (*e.g. iustitia,*

Gerechtigkeit). 'Righteousness' tends to suggest personal moral qualities, where 'justice' suggests a due care and concern for social issues. The Hebrew and Greek words underlying the Old and New Testaments do not allow this distinction to be made. Thus, in talking about the 'righteousness of God' (*e.g.*, Romans 1:17), Paul is embracing *both* 'righteousness' *and* 'justice'.

25. Mark 15:37–38.

26. Isaiah 53:10–12; 1 Peter 2:24.

27. Isaiah 53:12. Note how the gospel accounts of the crucifixion gently draw out the fact that Jesus was executed between two criminals. Here was the fulfilment of this prophecy.

28. 1 John 4:9–10.

29. For some of the problems, see Alister E. McGrath, *Iustitia Dei: A History of the Christian Doctrine of Justification* (2 vols.: Cambridge: Cambridge University Press, 1986), vol. 1, pp. 4–16.

30. Luke 1:68, King James Version.

31. C. S. Lewis, *God in the Dock* (Grand Rapids: Eerdmans, 1970), p. 96.

32. See Luke 7:36–50. Note the theme of 'Jesus the friend of sinners', formulated a few verses earlier (Luke 7:34).

33. John 3:16; Romans 5:8; 1 John 4:9–10. The argument at Romans 5:7–8 is especially revealing. Paul argues along the following lines. For someone to give his life for another is astonishing. Now we could begin to understand why someone should lay down his life for another person, if that person was really wonderful. That makes some kind of sense. But for someone to lay down his life for sinners – well, that is just amazing. Perhaps we need to put the 'amazing' back into 'grace'!

34. More accurately, a 'type'.

35. Mark 8:31; 9:12; 9:31; 10:33. Note the bewilderment of the disciples at 9:32, and Peter's refusal to accept Jesus' predictions of his suffering and death at 8:32–33.

36. Note also the declaration that Christ 'gave himself as a ransom for all' (1 Timothy 2:6).

37. Note the reworking of this theme at Luke 7:36–50, especially at verse 43. The point here is that the greater the debt that is cancelled, the greater our love for the one who cancelled the debt.

38. Note the use made of this point by Paul at 1 Corinthians 6:19–20 and 7:23.

39. In fact, the New International Version translates this same verb in this way at a number of major points – see Mark 5:23, 28, 34; 6:56; Luke 13:14; 18:42.

40. For the full implications of this approach for Christian spirituality, see Alister McGrath, *Roots that Refresh: A Celebration of Reformation Spirituality* (London: Hodder and Stoughton, 1992), chapters 8 and 9.

41. See especially 1 Corinthians 1:26–29.

42. For exploration of this point about doubt, see Alister McGrath, *Doubt: Handling it Honestly* (Leicester: Inter-Varsity Press, 1990). Doubt is *not* inconsistent with faith!

43. The interested reader may like to follow up this point with reference to Bertell Ollman, *Alienation* (Cambridge: Cambridge University Press, 1976).

44. Students of Marx will, course, realize that Marx recognizes a number of categories within each of these types of alienation – for example, there are four main categories of what I have here designated 'objective alienation' (*Entfremdung*).

45. Matthew 18:23–35 is a superb illustration of this

pressure, and its theological implications.

46. For a discussion of the relation of doctrine and feelings, see Alister McGrath, *Understanding Doctrine* (London: Hodder and Stoughton, 1991), pp. 39–52.

47. Two books are worth noting here. At an advanced level, see Os Guinness, *Doubt* (Tring: Lion, 1979); at a more popular level, see Alister McGrath, *Doubt: Handling it Honestly* (Leicester: Inter-Varsity Press, 1990).

48. Philippians 1:6.

49. The reader interested in these references to sixteenth-century reformers might like to explore Alister McGrath, *Roots that Refresh: A Celebration of Reformation Spirituality* (London: Hodder and Stoughton, 1992).

50. A central Pauline idea. To be 'in Christ' is to be united with and transformed by Christ. See 2 Corinthians 5:17 for a classic statement of this point.

51. John 5:3–6.

52. On this latter point, see Kenneth E. Bailey, *Poet and Peasant* (Grand Rapids: Eerdmans, 1976).

53. The reader wishing to know more about this notion might like to read R. Schacht, *Alienation* (New York: Doubleday, 1970).